THE
ENERGIZED
ENTERPRISE

THE ENERGIZED ENTERPRISE

How to Tap Your Organization's Hidden Potential

Fatima,
all the best !

marc

MARC G. STROHLEIN

iUniverse, Inc.
Bloomington

The Energized Enterprise
How to Tap Your Organization's Hidden Potential

iUniverse books may be ordered through booksellers or by contacting:

iUniverse
1663 Liberty Drive
Bloomington, IN 47403
www.iuniverse.com
1-800-Authors (1-800-288-4677)

ISBN: 978-1-4759-5932-1 (sc)
ISBN: 978-1-4759-5933-8 (ebk)

Printed in the United States of America

iUniverse rev. date: 11/15/2012

TABLE OF CONTENTS

Figures vii
Acknowledgements ix
Preface xi
About This Book xiii

Chapter 1.   The Eight Engines of the Energized Enterprise 1
Chapter 2.   Smart Work Habits 9
Chapter 3.   Compelling Purpose 25
Chapter 4.   Focused Leadership 40
Chapter 5.   Engaged Employees 53
Chapter 6.   Customer Intimacy 66
Chapter 7.   Dynamic Culture 80
Chapter 8.   Enterprise Collaboration 94
Chapter 9.   Transformational Technology 109
Chapter 10. Now It's Your Turn: Start Your Engines 125

About the Author 131

FIGURES

Figure 1: The Asymptotic Journey xiv

Figure 2: Moving from Enervated to Energized 3

Figure 3: IT Causal Loop Diagram...13

Figure 4: Agile Cycles 16

Figure 5: Lean Principles..20

Figure 6: Mission, Vision, Values, and Purpose.................................28

Figure 7: Priorities Versus Performance...43

Figure 8: MoSCoW for Setting Agile Priorities 49

Figure 9: From Buyers to Co-Creators..74

Figure 10: Strong and Weak Culture Comparison 82

Figure 11: Forces Behind Enterprise Collaboration 96

Figure 12: Hierarchical vs. Collaborative Communication 98

Figure 13: Shifting Business Challenges 99

Figure 14: Collaboration Tools..101

Figure 15: Principles of Collaboration..101

Figure 16: Stages of Business and Technology Strategy:
Functional View...114

Figure 17: Business and Technology Strategy:
Stages of Maturity 115

Figure 18: Employee Needs in Energized
Enterprise Achievement 126

Figure 19: The Virtuous Circle of Energizing Engines...................128

ACKNOWLEDGEMENTS

I'd like to list the many people and organizations that both inspired and contributed examples to this book, but they are too numerous to name (and some would likely prefer to remain anonymous).

I thank the many people who worked in my organizations over the years, as they provided the crucible where I forged many of the ideas described in this book as well as the energy to write it.

Special thanks to Brenda Newmann, who, to borrow from Michelangelo, patiently and skillfully sculpted a book from my text by removing all the parts that weren't "the book," and also contributed a number of critical suggestions that made this book what it is.

Finally, many thanks go to my wife, Patricia. Over the years, we've shared stories about the countless ups and downs in corporate life. Many of those experiences and the lessons learned are incorporated here. She also critiqued my thinking and reshaped some of my obscure references to avoid unnecessary head-scratching on your part.

PREFACE

Imagine a workplace where the air crackles with positive energy.

Employees feel they are on a meaningful mission, supported by management. Customers interact regularly with managers and employees. And managers are upbeat because they run a successful operation.

Sounds great, doesn't it? It's what I call an *energized enterprise.*

Energized enterprises have learned new ways of thinking and working that create a value trifecta of happy and productive employees, delighted customers, and profitable revenue.

They're also rare.

The good news is that these new ways of thinking and working are achievable for most, if not all, organizations. Better yet, they can be achieved without spending boatloads of money.

This book will show you how to use these new ways of thinking and working to unlock latent or hidden performance potential in your business or organization, no matter its size or goals—and without massive investments of money or resources.

Whether you're a top executive, division manager, or team leader, this book is a pragmatic and straightforward guide to tools and techniques for converting your organization's potential energy into the real thing.

In writing this book I drew on my experiences and observations over a 30-year career working for and with dozens of organizations, from start-up companies to global enterprises to non-profit organizations and associations. The common theme was that something was missing despite the presence of solid talent, technology, and management.

Here's why: enterprises comprise strategy, people, technology, and processes. But simply optimizing each of those elements—for example, by hiring the best people, buying the latest and best technology, and hiring the best consultants to streamline your processes—does not guarantee success.

Ignoring or mismanaging the interactions and interconnections between the elements leads to untapped potential energy and can cause unintended consequences when fixing a problem in one area leads to even bigger problems in another.

The result: conditions that drag down organizational performance.

This book will help you find that "something missing" in your organization and help you create your own energized enterprise.

This book should convince you of three things:

1. Your organization or enterprise has hidden and untapped performance potential that can be harnessed by applying a systematic approach to change.

2. You can tap that performance via eight "engines" that are straightforward and attainable by any organization.

3. Becoming an energized enterprise results in more productive and innovative employees, more loyal and profitable customers, and revenue growth that meets the goals of stakeholders.

It's a simple list, and this book will show that simplicity is pure gold when it comes to energizing enterprises.

ABOUT THIS BOOK

Over my career, I've been intrigued by the differences in energy levels, productivity, and success between "energized enterprises" and their anemic counterparts.

As I wrote this book, several people asked why I chose the word "energized." The answer is that I've worked with many organizations that were good, or even great, but lacked that intangible factor that motivates a person to get up in the morning raring to go. The best word I could find to describe that was "energy." Moreover, I kept finding overlooked opportunities to boost energy and performance—many at low or no cost.

In writing this book I relied more on direct experience and observation, and less on research, than some other business books. I also did not attempt to find companies that exemplify application of all eight engines, because I view energizing an enterprise as an ongoing journey for most organizations. An energized enterprise is a goal that is asymptotic in nature. If you are scratching your head, think back to high school math. An asymptotic curve is one where the gap between the curve and the line approaches, but does not reach, zero.

Figure 1: The Asymptotic Journey

Energized

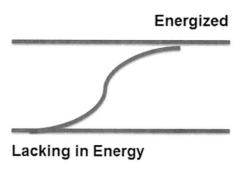

Lacking in Energy

Few, if any, organizations will ever hit the fully energized mark, but the process of working toward it will result in a better, continually improving organization, and that justifies the time and energy that you invest.

Goals for This Book

I had three goals in writing this book:

1. After many years of reading business books that talk *about* companies and *why* they are successful, I wanted to go further and provide the *how-to*. This book gives advice you can act on and, where appropriate, suggests tools and practices that can help achieve that energized state.

2. I am a big fan of continuous learning, so I provide suggested resources at the end of each chapter in hopes that you will continue the journey by taking advantage of some of the wisdom I tapped to write this book.

3. Finally, and most importantly, I wanted to help executives and managers think differently and take a systems view of the interconnections and interactions of the elements of their organizations.

Definitions and Disclosure

I use the terms "organization" and "enterprise" interchangeably throughout the book, and in the broadest sense, to include not only traditional for-profit businesses but also associations, government, educational institutions, and non-profits; in effect, any group—big or small—of people organized around a mission.

I recognize that some readers are CEOs and top executives, while others are team leaders or business-unit heads within a larger organization. Some conclusions and strategies will be very different for these two groups, and I've tried to make both feel at home here by including separate conclusions and "to-do lists" for each role at the end of Chapters 2-9—the eight engines.

In the spirit of full disclosure: I am a consultant who does not adhere to any particular methods, practices, or paradigms—I use and recommend what is appropriate for a given situation. That means I borrow from a number of sources and freely mash up practices to achieve the results I'm after. I've watched too many organizations slavishly adopt programs like Six Sigma, ISO 2000, or CMM and do a fabulous job of implementing the discipline but fail to gain the results they sought. I draw from a number of practices throughout the book, and they are all identified.

It has been said that the journey is its own reward, and I believe that the journey to an energized enterprise has many rewards. By the time you finish reading this book, I hope you'll agree and even embark on your own journey.

CHAPTER 1

THE EIGHT ENGINES

OF THE ENERGIZED ENTERPRISE

Energize—To give energy to; activate or invigorate.

Enterprises are like cars. They come in all sizes and shapes and with a wide range of engines and horsepower. They also need regular tune-ups and careful driving so they can perform at their peak.

Many of us have had the unfortunate experience of renting a car that turned out to be a "gutless wonder"—it looked spiffy on the lot, but after you turned into traffic and saw a speeding semi-trailer looming in the rear-view mirror, you realized the car lacked oomph. (Let's hope the semi had good brakes.)

You may be in a similar situation with your enterprise or organization. You've hired the best people you could find. You've bought the technology they said they needed to succeed. You've even brought in consultants and trainers to "tune up" their skills. Yet, when you need the organization to rise to the occasion, it reacts like that rental car—it lacks oomph.

Your team or organization has potential—probably a lot more than it currently exhibits. In fact, I believe that hidden in your organization, as in many others, lies an energized enterprise. And I'm going to show you strategies to uncover it.

1

This chapter introduces what I call the Eight Engines of Energized Enterprises, followed by data to back up their importance.

Defining the Energized Enterprise

Energized enterprises are "1+1=3" organizations. They optimize, align, and balance their strategies, people, processes, and technology—and, importantly, the *interactions* of those elements—so that the whole is greater than the sum of its parts. In contrast are *enervated* or de-energized organizations, which lack vigor and sometimes can feel like black holes where energy is sucked in but never released. They plod along, managing to stay alive, but are punching below their weight, ripe for disruption or even annihilation from more energized competitors.

Figure 2 compares these two kinds of enterprises. Most of the differences relate to ways of thinking and doing, which means you don't need to invest massive sums of money to move from enervated to energized.

Figure 2: Moving from Enervated to Energized

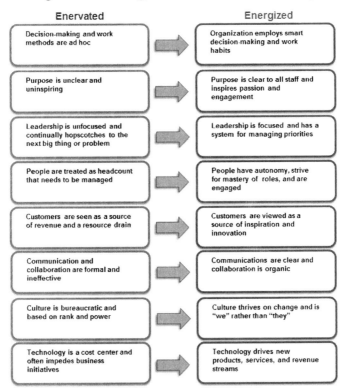

Myriad factors contribute to performance (or non-performance) of organizations. I'll focus on eight that I call the engines of an energized enterprise, summarized here and explored further in subsequent chapters.

1. **Smart Work Habits**. Energized enterprises continually examine what's working and what's not, and refine their ways of thinking and acting. They use continuous learning and iterative refinement to keep the organization growing and improving. Energized enterprises work smarter, not harder.

2. **Compelling Purpose**. These enterprises have a higher calling, and their purpose is clear, important, and known to all employees, customers, and partners. Strategies, goals, and resources are

aligned from top to bottom, and every employee can explain the enterprise's mission and how their role contributes to it.

3. **Focused Leadership**. Leaders know how to figure out what is important and what is not, and how to stay focused on the former. Leaders focus on delivering value to customers and manage priorities in pursuit of that aim.

4. **Engaged Employees**. Employees are not merely empowered; they have autonomy and are highly engaged in mastering their roles and delivering value to their customers.

5. **Customer Intimacy**. Customers are viewed as a wellspring of innovation and energy. They are seen not as a revenue source or support drain but as collaborators and co-creators of value.

6. **Dynamic Culture**. Leaders and employees take joint ownership and accountability for success. Employees and managers say "we," not "I" or "they." The culture embraces change and thrives on success and customer satisfaction.

7. **Enterprise Collaboration**. Leaders focus on clearly communicating goals and on creating an environment where collaboration happens naturally and effectively. Employees work together in cross-functional teams to maximize achievement.

8. **Transformational Technology**. Technology not only enables the business mission and purpose but also drives it forward. Technology is not seen as a cost center but rather as a source of innovation, customer delight, and new revenue.

Notably, these engines aren't specific to any type or size of organization—they apply equally well to teams, departments, start-ups, non-profits, government and educational organizations, and global businesses. I selected them for this book because they are equal opportunity engines.

In my experience, fully energized enterprises are scarce. Many, perhaps most, of the organizations I have encountered fall somewhere on the continuum from enervated to energized. They may have some energized elements, but they lack others and are simply not performing at their peak.

The biggest reason I have found that companies have hidden, untapped performance potential is that they focus on individual components—people, technology, processes, etc.—instead of taking a "systems view" that optimizes the components *and* their interactions. That is where the untapped potential lies, and it's why Chapter 2 contains a discussion of systems thinking.

Why Get Energized?

With all the priorities facing leaders and managers, it's tempting to ask why creating an energized enterprise should be a priority, let alone at the top of the heap. It's tempting to keep bumping along, fixing things here and there and hoping for a bit of magic. After all, change is hard and can be perilous.

But, consider this: I believe that failure to move from enervated to energized will, over the long term, be an organization's death knell.

Today's business environment really is "the best of times" and "the worst of times," to borrow from Charles Dickens.

Better technology, smarter workers, broader opportunities to make money, and a potential customer base that grows along with the population all point toward better times, despite a challenging economy.

But turbulent, unpredictable, and predatory business environments, fickle customers with dwindling attention spans, disengaged and footloose employees, and nimble and merciless competition make it a challenging time to be in business.

Contradictory? Not if your organization is an energized enterprise.

Here are some statistics about each of the eight engines to back me up:

Smart Work Habits. A 2011 IBM study showed that high-performing organizations were three times as likely as medium-performing organizations to use what it calls "smart work methods." In other words, they are continually honing and refining not only what they do but also how they do it. IBM is a great example of a company that uses smart work methods including agile (discussed in Chapter 2) and social collaboration (Chapter 8) to drive performance.

Compelling Purpose. Success Profiles, a performance management company, studied 600 businesses and found that the average profit per employee in the survey increased from $7,802 to $27,401 in companies that make clear communication of their mission and values a best practice. In other words, having a clear and compelling mission or purpose pays.

Focused Leadership. A 2011 Booz & Company survey showed the following results:

- 53% of surveyed executives said they don't believe their own strategies will lead to success.

- 64% said their company has too many conflicting priorities.

- 49% said their company lacks even a list of strategic priorities.

- 54% said their employees and customers don't understand how the company creates value.

Those are appalling numbers, but they square with what I've observed in my professional experience. In fact, I've seen more than a few companies where the management team seems to revel in chaos because it cements their roles as "deciders." On a more positive note, the same survey showed that organizations that pursue fewer priorities perform better than those that pursue many.

Engaged Employees. A 2011 BlessingWhite study found that only 49% of responding employees agreed that their executives have created a work environment that drives strong performance. Surveys of employee engagement levels show similarly depressing statistics. The good news is that this can be turned around, and a 2010 study by Hewitt Associates found that high-engagement firms exhibited shareholder returns 19% higher than average.

Customer Intimacy. A study by The American Management Association in conjunction with the Institute for Corporate Productivity found that 70% of high-performing companies put focus on creating customer-focused cultures. Customer intimacy isn't a job or a chore—it's a core competency for energized enterprises.

Dynamic Culture. Harvard professors John Kotter and James Heskett, in their 1992 book *Corporate Culture and Performance*, found that firms with shared-values-based cultures enjoyed 400% higher revenues, 700% greater job growth, 1,200% higher stock prices and significantly faster profit performance than other companies in similar industries. Yvon Chouinard has commented that every time his company, Patagonia, does the right thing, it turns out to be good business.

Enterprise Collaboration. An MIT study found that employees with the most extensive digital (collaborative) networks were 7% more productive than their colleagues.

Transformational Technology. The Harvard Business Review states that companies that manage their IT assets well get returns as much as 40% higher than their competitors that don't. Imagine the lift your organization could see with that kind of technology leverage!

These are just a few reasons why finding that inner energized enterprise in your organization is important, and arguably necessary for survival. Old ways of organizing and working won't fly. Most enterprises use organization structures and management approaches that were designed for the industrial economy and slightly updated for the services economy but are totally inadequate for the digital economy.

Change management that takes months and years is too slow. Reorganizing the company every time a new threat or opportunity arises won't work. Hiring new skill sets every time something changes in the marketplace is doomed to fail. And most of all, current approaches to hierarchical command and control management will not give organizations the agility, flexibility, and drive that they need.

What's needed is a new way of thinking, organizing, and working that taps into the hidden energy lying within most organizations. The following chapters examine the roots of sub-par performance in each engine and recommend ways to move from enervated to energized, starting with working smarter in Chapter 2.

Resources

- BlessingWhite Research. 2011. *Employee Engagement Report 2011*. BlessingWhite Inc.

- Collins, Jim. 2001. *Good to Great.* Harper Collins.

- IBM Study. April, 2011. *The New Workplace: Are You Ready?* IBM Corporation.

- Kotter, John P., and James L. Heskett. 1992. *Corporate Culture and Performance.* Free Press.

- Olivo, Tom. 2009. *Improving The Health of Healthcare One Organization at a Time.* Success Profiles, Inc.

- Sisodia, Rajendri, David B. Wolfe, and Jagdish N. Sheth. 2007. *Firms of Endearment.* Pearson Prentice Hall.

CHAPTER 2

SMART WORK HABITS

The combination of hard work and smart work is efficient work"—Robert Half

Prime the Engine: Pre-Reading Questions

Each chapter about the eight engines begins with a set of questions to orient your thinking before you dive into the main content. As you read them, consider how the material applies to your organization and which concepts or practices are most useful to you. Here are questions for this chapter:

1. Does your management team devote time to discussing the practices and methods used to get work done across the entire enterprise?

2. Are standard methods used for managing projects, developing products, handling customer issues, and other business activities?

3. Do managers and employees have a clear view of value from a customer's standpoint, and their own role in delivering value?

4. When things go wrong, is there a larger investigation into root causes instead of simply finding people at fault?

If you answered "no" to any of these, then read on—this chapter will help you turn nos into yesses.

Introduction

Most of us are already working hard, but as demands on us grow, we need to get better at working smart—as individuals and especially as organizations. I'm talking about enterprises that take a disciplined approach not only to determining what they do, but *how* they do it. This chapter focuses on the "how."

For many organizations, decision-making, processes, and work methods are unruly and ad hoc. Often, they emerge from the past lives of employees—the dreaded "in my last company we did it this way" approach. These methods and processes may have worked elsewhere but are often ill-suited for new environments.

Energized enterprises pay attention to how decisions are made and how things get done. They use a flexible tool kit of practices and principles to extract maximum performance from project teams and operations staff. In this chapter, I focus on three such practices or disciplines: systems thinking, agile development, and lean production. I chose these because their interlocking principles make them more powerful together than they are apart. There's that 1+1=3 equation again!

This chapter distills key concepts that can be applied in the pursuit of tapping hidden performance. I cherry-picked the ideas that are applicable in the context of this book and left out those that aren't. These are tools and techniques to get things done—not dogma—so use them to help solve your problems and not to remain faithful to the "rules."

Volumes have been written about each of these disciplines, so I don't claim that this book will fully explain them or make you an expert. I encourage you to further explore these topics later, starting with the list of sources at the end of the chapter.

Systems Thinking: Don't Be a Balloon Squeezer

Organizations are systems, and in systems a change in one part often leads to changes in others. These changes are unanticipated and often unwelcome. For example, taking the sales team to a "well deserved" boondoggle in Aspen may improve their morale but will also lead to an equal or greater morale drop for the folks who supported sales but didn't get to go.

Promotions are a particularly volatile systems event because they lead to subtle power and relationship shifts that can confound even seasoned managers. For the newly promoted, the shock of going from esteemed peer to pointy-haired boss can be a life-changing experience—and not a good one.

For many managers, systems thinking is an esoteric and even academic discipline to be avoided at all costs. To them I say, "avoid systems thinking at your own peril." The reason is that actions often lead to unforeseen and unintended consequences elsewhere in the system. Just ask the newly minted pointy-haired boss. His promotion could lead to his being shunned by former peers or even falling prey to the Peter Principle and realizing he's not up to the new job.

Many proponents of systems thinking say that you need to be steeped in the theory and doctrine in order to use it effectively, and that it is an all-or-nothing proposition. Don't believe them. The key is simply to recognize that organizations are complex systems that contain other systems. Changes in one part of a system lead to changes in other parts of the system or even in other systems. Unforeseen changes lead to unintended consequences. If you've ever squeezed a balloon at one end only to have it go "pop" at the other, you know what I'm talking about.

Energized-enterprise leaders see not only the components that make up their organizations but also the interplay and interactions that make them perform. They employ systems thinking to make decisions that take those interactions into account.

What Is Systems Thinking?

Systems thinking as a discipline has its foundations in the field of systems dynamics, founded in 1956 by MIT professor Jay Forrester. But the roots of systems thinking go back more than 2,000 years, to Aristotle's *Metaphysica*: "Now anything that has a plurality of parts but is not just the sum of these, like a heap, but exists as a whole beyond its parts, invariably has a cause."

Traditional analytical thinking focuses on identifying and isolating the individual pieces of what's being studied in order to examine them in further detail. In contrast, systems thinking focuses on the interactions of the pieces, or elements, that make up a system. In other words, the traditional analysis that most organizations do before making decisions focuses on the details of a single element, whereas systems thinking expands outward to understand how that element interacts with others in the organization.

Donella Meadows, author of *Limits to Growth*, also wrote the excellent *Thinking in Systems: A Primer*, where she defines a system as "an interconnected set of elements that is coherently organized in a way that achieves something." Systems can be simple, such as a thermostat, or they can be quite complex, like an enterprise, which consists of subsystems within systems and many forms of interconnections.

Drawing from Meadows' *Thinking in Systems* book, systems consist of elements that can include the following:

- Inputs: energy and resources that flow into a system

- Outputs: energy and resources that flow out of a system

- Stocks: reservoirs fed by inputs and drained by outputs that slow the reaction of a system

- Feedback or causal loops: information flows that control and constrain or grow and exaggerate behaviors in a system (the first is a negative loop; the second, positive)

12

- Constraints: controls and limits on the behavior of individual components

A system's elements are organized to achieve a purpose. Figure 3 describes a fairly simple system for an application development group in IT trying to keep up with work requests from business units and produce finished applications (this system's purpose).

Figure 3: IT Causal Loop Diagram

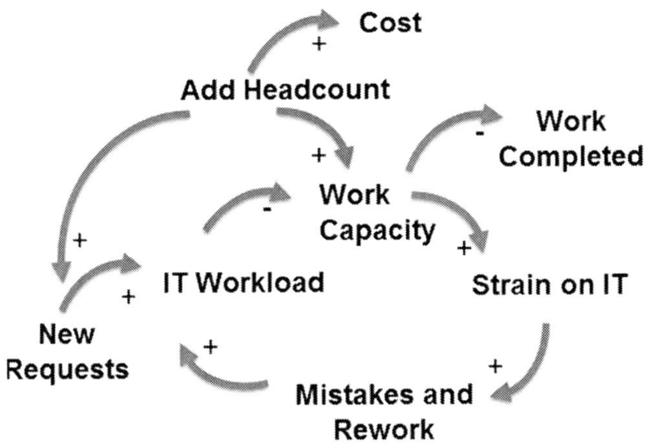

Let's look at an example of applying systems thinking to solve a problem—the IT application development group's inability to keep up with work requests. I've used a common diagramming approach that depicts causal loops that indicate both the linkages between elements of a system and whether their impact is to control and constrain (minus sign) or grow and exaggerate (plus sign).

When IT organizations get overloaded with work, their performance drops, they make mistakes, and the result is an increase in rework. That, in turn, leads to a higher workload, which reduces IT's work capacity. This is a pretty common scenario, and many organizations take the obvious approach of adding more IT headcount.

But because adding headcount leads to higher work capacity (the "+" on the arrow from "add headcount" to "work capacity,") business units often increase the number of work requests (the "+" on the arrow from "add headcount" to "new requests"). That increased work capacity erodes quickly in the face of new requests. The diagram helps by revealing that adding headcount has both positive and negative consequences and by showing other possible actions to relieve the situation. These include adding better governance to limit new requests to those that most positively impact the business, and adding better quality assurance capabilities to reduce mistakes and rework.

Your takeaway, as a reader of this book, is the following:

In making organizational and other changes, it is important to view the elements and interconnections that make up the system(s) targeted for change. And, to the extent possible, try to model or think about how the planned change will affect other parts of the organization. It has been said that every complex problem has a simple answer; unfortunately, that answer is usually wrong. Systems thinking helps managers avoid the simple-answer trap.

I've illustrated one example, but systems thinking can be applied to decisions ranging from pricing adjustments to reporting relationship realignment to changes in customer service policies, to name just a few.

Why Systems Thinking Works

Organizations often adopt point solutions aimed at fixing a problem, but these inadvertently cause other issues. This leads to the "squeezing the balloon" phenomenon, where a change in one part of the organization breaks something in another part. A management team can easily become consumed by balloon squeezing while the rest of the organization suffers the consequences. Become a systems thinker, not a balloon squeezer.

Agile Thinking: Not Just for Software Anymore

I first ran across the "agile" concept in 2002 and was intrigued by a software development process that actually embraced changes in business requirements. Dealing with change has been anathema to developers for decades and a real thorn in the side of business managers who have to cope with volatile business environments.

But agile isn't just for software development. It's a basic project management approach and a way of thinking that can be applied to many types of projects and initiatives with solid results. Consider research by IBM and BTM Research showing that companies with "very mature business agility characteristics exhibited superior financial performance," including:

- 13-38% higher capital efficiency and value

- 10-15% higher margins

- 0.2-5% higher revenue and earnings growth

Getting agile pays!

What Is Agile?

While most agile literature focuses on practices, I also like to talk about agile "thinking." The linear forms of thinking that most organizations use are rooted in a time when the world was a somewhat linear and predictable place. That's no longer true, and the "research → plan → build → test → launch" approach doesn't work very well in volatile environments.

What's the alternative? An agile approach that uses a series of loops, where each loop builds on the previous ones, as in Figure 4.

Figure 4: Agile Cycles

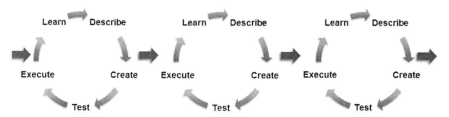

Agile works by breaking big efforts into small pieces, each of which constitutes a full project cycle. Agile development starts with a light set of requirements and a high-level architecture (or definition of desired outcomes). These are enough to understand the scope of the project and to get started, but they aren't a comprehensive set of requirements.

Once team members complete high-level requirements, they start a series of iterations, or cycles, that are usually 2-4 weeks long. Each iteration encompasses description, design, development, testing, and "launch" of a working subset of the product that can be reviewed by stakeholders. When stakeholders agree that they have enough of these subsets to make up a critical mass of functionality and content, the product can be launched or the project is complete.

Many organizations have embraced agile software development over the past several years, and I believe that some of the same core principles and practices should be applied in other areas of enterprises to get things done faster, better, and more energetically. Specifically, breaking big projects into smaller pieces, using iterations to check assumptions, and testing and learning continually are all broadly applicable in project management.

Agile can be a great fit in a project or initiative with any of the following characteristics: the desired outcome is not known in great detail; needs and requirements may, or will likely, change; completion will require an extended effort; or close cooperation is needed between workers and stakeholders. In today's chaotic business environments, many—if not most—projects and initiatives fit that description.

Why Agile Works

Agile works because it appeals to human nature.

First, cycle times are short. Most people crave a sense of accomplishment, and because of its short iterations, agile fills that need in spades. With every iteration, some tasks are completed.

Second, agile is transparent and self-reinforcing. Managers find agile stand-up meetings liberating as they put each team member's efforts in plain sight. Underperformance becomes a team issue, not a management headache.

Third, agile is fun! Agile managers I've talked to say this is what they like best about it, and I agree. Most of my favorite projects during my career have been agile. Agile gives team members a chance to shine and gain recognition from both teammates and customers.

What Is Lean?

While I've never formally practiced "lean," over the years I've found some of its principles useful in problem-solving and reducing inefficiency. Lean is a production practice that views resource expenditure for any goal other than creating customer value as wasteful and a target for elimination. "Value" is defined as any action or process that a customer would be willing to pay for; in other words, value is in the eye of the customer. Essentially, lean is centered on preserving value with less work.

For our purposes, I'm taking a broad view of both customers and value: customers are not only external actors that receive value for payment, but also internal customers that don't directly pay for services or value they receive. For the former, think of a customer buying a car, and for the latter, a finance organization getting a new automated data report generated by the IT department.

Lean thinking emerged in the post-World War II reconstruction of Japan's economy and manufacturing base, spurred by work done by W. Edwards Deming, the American business management expert, and more fully realized in Toyota's production systems. Lean was in large part responsible for the resurgence of Japanese industry and a subsequent wake-up call to US industry.

While the roots of lean are in manufacturing, many of the concepts are highly adaptable to other areas of an enterprise. In fact, agile development draws heavily from lean, although agile is team-focused while lean helps scale across an entire enterprise.

To be precise, the concept of "lean" is comprised of lean thinking, or philosophy, and lean principles, which are the embodiment of lean thinking. Here are some examples of lean thinking drawn from lean software development thought-leader Alan Shalloway in his book, *Lean-Agile Software Development*:

- Most errors are due to the system within which people work rather than to the individuals themselves.

- People doing the work are the best ones to understand how to improve the system, and management must work with teams to improve the way they work and increase their efficiency.

- Ad hoc is not an acceptable process.

- Teams are most efficient when the amount of work is limited to their capacity and work-in-progress is minimized.

- When evaluating actions, we must optimize the whole process, not merely improve individual steps.

Lean dovetails with systems thinking in considering that errors are systemic and remediation needs to focus on the system in which they occur, not the people who make the mistakes. It also ties in with agile in the idea of work being done in small batches and limited to the capacity of the team or organization, and in focusing on delivery of value to customers.

Now that we've looked at examples of lean thinking, here are the five core lean principles highlighted in *Lean Thinking* by James P. Womack and Daniel T. Jones:

1. Value is specified from the customer's point of view. Anything that does not add value should be minimized or eliminated.

2. Value stream maps identify all the steps in a process and define them in three categories: value-add, non-value-add but necessary, and non-value-add and unnecessary.

3. Process steps are arranged in a flow with tight sequencing.

4. Workers in a process flow pull work from the preceding activity; it's not pushed to them. This means that work at one stage is completed when the result or product of that work is needed at the next stage, not before or after. That minimizes the need for re-work due to changing needs, as well as bottlenecks and delays.

5. Pursuit of perfection never ends.

Figure 5 illustrates the fact that lean, like agile, employs cycles.

Figure 5: Lean Principles

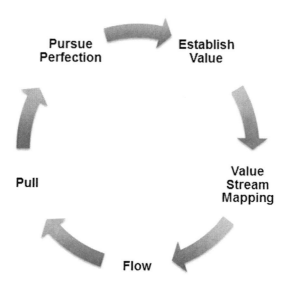

Pursue Perfection → **Establish Value** → **Value Stream Mapping** → **Flow** → **Pull** →

A study by Cardiff Business School highlights the role of customer value as a focal point in energized enterprises. The study showed that only 5% of a typical business's production operations are activities that directly add customer value, 35% are non-value-adding but necessary, and an astounding 60% of activities add no value and are unnecessary.

I'll note here that working on activities that add no discernable value is not very engaging, something we'll explore in Chapter 5. Employees can generally sense when their work has no intrinsic value, so imagine the loss of energy that occurs in a firm where 60% of employee time and resources are applied to performing such activities!

Why Lean Works

Lean thinking works because it puts decision-making in the hands of those who know best how to fix and optimize processes, it depersonalizes problem solving, and it helps take the emotion out of resolving issues. It also helps lower stress by reducing the mountainous backlogs of work that loom over most organizations.

Most importantly, a ruthless focus on eliminating non-value-adding activities is both a cost-saver and tremendously liberating to an organization. Nobody comes to work eagerly anticipating doing a job that adds no discernible value to anything.

For CEOs and Executives

For executives, this chapter is the "heavy lifting" part of this book. Embracing and using these practices and ways of thinking will require some effort beyond reading this chapter. Yet tackling any of them will yield significant benefits, and collectively they can transform your enterprise into a lean, agile, and optimized organization. I think that's worth some quality time and energy. Here are my recommendations for you:

- Don't overreach by trying to adopt all of these disciplines at once. Focus on identifying opportunities to apply smart work habits to solve important business needs and problems in your organization.

- Don't succumb to the temptation to hire experts to do the heavy lifting. Start by talking to people in your IT, product development, and production groups. You may have a wealth of knowledge about agile, lean, and systems thinking already in your organization.

- Divide and conquer—if you decide to tackle two or three of these disciplines, assign owners who can create Centers of Excellence (COE) for each one. COEs are small teams that are the "go to" source for each discipline and can be a resource to teams or departments in implementing them.

- If you pick only one discipline, make it systems thinking. Lack of systems thinking is a big challenge and detriment to most enterprises, and adopting it will save you from many mistakes while helping you focus resources on what matters.

For Team Leaders and Business Unit Managers

While the CEO has the immense task of figuring out how to leverage these disciplines from the top down, you have the relative luxury of working on a smaller, though no less important, scale. You also have a great opportunity to demonstrate success with these disciplines and become a thought leader. Here's what I recommend for you:

- Look for opportunities to apply one or more of these practices within your own organization. Start small, but pick applications that matter and provide business value.

- Become an owner of a Center of Excellence. It could be a powerful springboard for your career and will encourage you to dig in and learn one or more of the disciplines.

- Get in the habit of asking yourself "what are the impacts and implications of this decision I am about to make?" If they appear potentially significant, spend some time creating a causal loop or other diagram to help understand them before making your decision.

Living Smart Work Habits

Going back to the IT example in Figure 3, let's see how systems thinking, agile, and lean can be used in concert to analyze and remedy the problem. Figure 3 shows that the obvious solution of adding headcount has drawbacks, including added costs and business units' expectations for more work to get done. It also makes clear that other points of leverage could solve the problem: the quality assurance (QA) function, efficiency of the development group, and governance that manages the work requests.

Agile development and the notions of cycles, product owners, and prioritized backlogs are prime candidates to help solve the IT governance conundrum. Because each agile iteration results in working code that the requestors and stakeholders get to see, it's not uncommon for an application to satisfy business needs before reaching a point where it addresses the original scope and requirements. The result is less work and the ability to move on to the next project.

Agile also helps formulate simple prioritization criteria to streamline the request queue. Using the measures of business impact and time-and-resource requirements, it is easy to put high-impact/ low-resource projects first, followed by low-impact/low resource and high-impact/high-resource projects, and drop low-impact/ high-resource projects altogether. Again, the result is less work for the IT organization with minimal impact on the business.

Lean thinking also plays a role in helping optimize this system. A review of most IT work queues will reveal that many IT projects have at best tenuous ties to external customer value, and even to internal customer value in some cases.

It is possible to make a big dent in the work backlog by eliminating the latter category and scrutinizing the former to make sure that the project requests at least fall into the "non-value-add but necessary" bucket. You can explain to stakeholders for the eliminated projects that their projects did not pass the customer-value test.

Using lean thinking's notion of value stream mapping, it is useful to look at the end-to-end process of generating IT project ideas through the delivery of finished applications. It is often possible to find (and eliminate) waste in the form of delays, sign-offs, hand-offs, waiting for interdependent projects to be completed, and so on.

Finally, it is important to engage IT staff assistance in redesigning the processes. Enlist them to help management and the governance council to understand the IT organization's capacity for work in order to develop a better framework for prioritizing projects. I've never met an IT team that doesn't have good ideas about the flow and prioritization of IT projects—they just aren't asked, and that is both demoralizing and a tremendous waste.

I've barely scratched the surface of systems thinking, lean, and agile, but I hope this chapter whets your appetite for more knowledge and that you'll take advantage of the resource list. In Chapter 3, we move on to clear and compelling purpose.

Resources

- Alman, David. 2011. *Using Systems Thinking to Improve Organizations.* Systems Thinking Approaches blog, October 27. http://systems-thinking-approaches.blogspot.com/

- Economist Intelligence Unit. March 2009. *Organizational Agility: How Businesses Can Survive and Thrive in Turbulent Times,* The Economist.

- Gabor, Andrea. 2010. *Seeing Your Company as a System.* May 25, Strategy+Business.

- Meadows, Donella. December 3, 2008. *Thinking in Systems.* Chelsea Green Publishing

- Ries, Eric. 2012. *The Lean Startup.* Crown Business

- Schwaber, Ken. 2004. *Agile Project Management With Scrum.* Microsoft Press.

- Shalloway, Alan, Guy Beaver, and James R. Trott. 2010. *Lean-Agile Software Development,* Pearson Education Inc.

- Sherwood, Dennis. August 27, 2002. *Seeing the Forest for the Trees: A Manager's Guide to Applying Systems Thinking.* Nicholas Brealey Publishing.

- Womack, James P. and Daniel T. Jones. 2003. *Lean Thinking.* Free Press.

CHAPTER 3

COMPELLING PURPOSE

"Efforts and courage are not enough without purpose and direction."—John F. Kennedy

"To forget one's purpose is the commonest form of stupidity."—Friedrich Nietzsche

Prime the Engine: Pre-Reading Questions

1. Do you have a clear view of your organization's purpose—why it exists? Do your employees understand and embrace that purpose?

2. Can employees explain how their jobs relate to the purpose of the greater organization?

3. Do employees cite the organization's purpose when discussing possible strategies and courses of action, or do the two seem disconnected and abstract?

4. Does your organization's purpose raise your energy level?

Ideally, your answers should be 1) yes, 2) yes, 3) yes/no, 4) yes. If not, the following chapter will help you get there.

Introduction

Systems of all types need a purpose, a *raison d'etre*, a reason to exist. People, companies, and teams without purpose are zombies. Actually, they're worse—even zombies have a purpose. Yet purpose can vary from unexciting and uninspiring all the way to galvanizing and exhilarating. Energized enterprises have figured out how to create and leverage purpose in order to focus and inspire their teams' performance while engaging customers.

Purpose on Purpose

> *"Purpose: the reason for which anything is done,*
> *is created, or exists."*

I'm reminded of an anecdotal story about President Kennedy visiting NASA's headquarters in 1961 and encountering a janitor. The president shook his hand and asked him what he did for NASA. The janitor replied, "Sir, I'm helping to put a man on the moon!" That is an example of clear and compelling purpose, understood and embraced far down in an organization.

Purpose is a compass that guides the activities of people and organizations. If your organization lacks a clear, well-understood purpose, your employees—unlike the janitor—will be unclear about how their jobs contribute to a "greater good." Just as people need a purpose for their existence, so do enterprises. Purpose matters, and it factors into an enterprise's performance.

In fact, having a clear purpose can pay off financially. "A strong, strategically coherent and well communicated purpose is associated with up to 17% better financial performance and builds trust with stakeholders," according to a 2010 study of 213 European firms by IMD, a leading business school, and Burson-Marsteller, a public relations firm. Beyond that, purpose defines who you are and dictates other aspects of organizational life including culture, standing in the business and local communities, and even who your employees are and how dedicated they will be.

Purpose is the heart and soul of an organization and a major catalyst for an energized enterprise. Who would want to work for an organization with an unclear purpose, or one at odds with their personal beliefs? Answer: those who are only in it for the money—precisely the sort of folks most organizations don't want to hire.

Paradoxically, some of the most dedicated workers I've met are volunteers. One way to learn about what a compelling purpose looks like is to volunteer at a non-profit, preferably in your community. In my experience, local non-profits tend to focus on delivering value to their constituency, and their purpose, even if not formally stated, emerges from their work. A simple, down-to-earth shared purpose is much more powerful than superlative-laden tomes.

Most organizations communicate their purpose through some combination of mission, vision, and values statements. I "purposely" left those words out of this chapter's title because something gets lost in translation when organizations try to create and use those artifacts.

In this chapter, I'll briefly discuss mission, vision, and values statements and why they can be counterproductive, and then try to convince you instead to focus on establishing a broader organizational "purpose" that permeates thoughts and actions.

Mission, Vision, and Values: Cornerstones or Millstones?

Over years of observing how organizations state their missions, visions, and values, I've been struck by the confusion surrounding the definitions and uses of these three words. What's more, the actual statements are all over the map and often of little use in determining an organization's true purpose.

I'll try to blow away these clouds of confusion by providing my own definitions of vision, mission, and values, and how purpose relates to them:

- Mission describes *what* the organization does.

- Vision is the *why* that describes a future desired state that (hopefully) arises from the organization's performance of its mission.

- Values are principles that guide *how* the organization behaves.

To those, I add a fourth, more powerful term: Purpose is the overarching *raison d'etre* that emerges from the confluence of mission, vision, and values along with the way in which an organization lives those statements, as shown in Figure 6.

Figure 6: Mission, Vision, Values, and Purpose

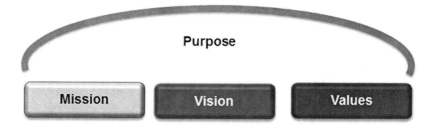

Purpose can replace mission, vision, and values statements, but it doesn't have to—in fact, it can amplify those statements to make them more memorable. What is important, regardless of the approach you take, is to make sure any statements are meaningful, compelling, and relevant, as well as understandable to all of your audiences.

First, let's look at some examples to illustrate the roots of my disaffection with these tools. Mission statements are the most common "statements" and a good place to begin.

When the Mission Becomes a Mission

A common mistake organizations make when trying to define their mission is that the statements are either so high-level and abstract that they are meaningless, or they are larded with everything but the kitchen sink. Most annoying are statements filled with superlatives. Take Sony's, for example, from its website:

> *"Sony is committed to developing a wide range of innovative products and multimedia services that challenge the way consumers access and enjoy digital entertainment. By ensuring synergy between businesses within the organization, Sony is constantly striving to create exciting new worlds of entertainment that can be experienced on a variety of different products."*

It may be sheer coincidence that, at the time of this writing, Sony is struggling in the marketplace, but perhaps not. This is a classic example of "let's start with words like innovative, synergy, exciting, striving, and experience, and create a mission statement." Worse yet, some of Sony's products do challenge the way I enjoy digital entertainment, but not in the way they intended.

Now take American Standard's mission statement:

> *"Be the best in the eyes of our customers, employees and shareholders."*

American Standard should have heeded Einstein's advice that "everything should be made as simple as possible, but not simpler." If you were an employee, how would this mission inform your approach to doing your work? As a manager, would this help you inspire the troops? What exactly is "the best"? This statement is too simple, generic, and vague.

Finally let's look at Disney's mission statement:

> *"The mission of The Walt Disney Company is to be one of the world's leading producers and providers of entertainment and*

information. Using our portfolio of brands to differentiate our content, services and consumer products, we seek to develop the most creative, innovative and profitable entertainment experiences and related products in the world."

That statement, while it doesn't "stir the soul," pretty well reflects what Disney is about and does it in an honest and straightforward way. Mission statements don't have to dazzle—they need to communicate what an organization does and what it is trying to be, and I think this statement fills the bill.

Where mission statements can go awry is when they clearly do not match the organization's behavior. Enron's "Respect, Integrity, Communication and Excellence" motto was clearly off the mark. Imagine the cognitive dissonance experienced by any employees who tried to live those values.

My beef with mission statements is that even when they are well crafted, they often seem like artifacts that have little or nothing to do with the organization in question. That's because they are often created using the services of high-priced consultants bearing gilded words and phrases, or by committees where seemingly each member gets to volunteer his or her favorite superlative.

The statements tend to reflect what management thinks the market wants the organization to be, not what management believes it is. This type of mission statement doesn't energize an enterprise—it can sap the energy right out of it.

That Vision Thing

Vision statements are an organization's view of its future—what it wants to be and how it wants to "change the world," or at least the lives of its customers. Like mission statements, vision statements often suffer from under- or overreach because their creation becomes disconnected from the organization's purpose and takes on a life of its own.

Despite my skepticism about vision statements, good ones do exist. One example is Harley Davidson's: *"Our key goal is to fulfill dreams through the experiences of motorcycling."* Short, sweet, and believable.

Not so good is Epson's vision:

> *"Epson is committed to the relentless pursuit of innovation in compact, energy-saving, high-precision technologies, and through the formation of group-wide platforms will become a community of robust businesses, creating, producing, and providing products and services that emotionally engage customers worldwide."*

Forgetting my puzzlement over what "group-wide platforms" are, this statement just sounds manufactured, much like the stuff that Epson sells. Nothing in it separates Epson from its high-tech competitors.

Note that the difference between these vision statements and the preceding mission statements is pretty small. In my research I found that many mission and vision statements seemed interchangeable, resulting in confusion over what they actually are. More importantly, they lack context and often seem to have little to do with the organizations that created them. That's because they reflect what management thinks the market wants to hear, not what management believes about its own organization.

Values: Where Dilbert Lives

While organizations can trip up on mission and vision statements, defining "values" can truly induce eye rolling and cynicism. Employees can generally ignore the mission and vision statements, but corporate values really hit home and can't be ignored. That's because values often include concepts that are readily observable by employees, such as "we value work/life balance," and "we believe in empowering employees to provide superior customer service." Those values need to be "lived" or they become a poke in the eye with a sharp stick for employees.

Unfortunately, many organizations do not live the values they espouse, and that is worse than having no stated values at all. Research by Edwin Giblin and Linda Amuso of Iquantic, Inc., done for California State University, found that corporate values have to be internalized by employees in order to have meaning, and that rarely happens.

There are lots of reasons for this. Most important is that enterprises, particularly public ones, continually confront changing circumstances that make adherence to core principles difficult, if not impossible. Giblin and Amuso use the example of a company that has espoused "putting the customer first" as a value, but then finds that a long-term customer has requested a pricing structure that forces the company to run a loss for some period of time. Despite the core value statement that "the very basis of our existence is customers," the company opts to instead "go for the money." That's a deal breaker for any truly conscientious employee.

Another problem, noted by Robert Jackall, professor of sociology and public affairs, is that leaders' and managers' "public language is best characterized as a kind of provisional discourse, a tentative way of communicating that reflects the peculiarly chancy and fluid character of their world." In other words, the very concept of fixed, core values is at odds with the way leaders think and communicate.

Our first values statement example comes from Microsoft and exemplifies the challenges associated with creating and living a strong set of core values:

> *"As a company, and as individuals, we value integrity, honesty, openness, personal excellence, constructive self-criticism, continual self-improvement, and mutual respect. We are committed to our customers and partners and have a passion for technology. We take on big challenges, and pride ourselves on seeing them through. We hold ourselves accountable to our customers, shareholders, partners, and employees by honoring our commitments, providing results, and striving for the highest quality."*

Imagine the challenge of living up to those values every day.

My advice is to pick simple, basic values that matter and that can generally be adhered to, such as respect, dignity, honesty, and fairness, for starters. Then make sure that the organization's leadership not only espouses the values but also lives them, visibly and continuously.

A second example returns to Enron. Its "Vision and Values" mission statement was surreal: *"We treat others as we would like to be treated ourselves. We do not tolerate abusive or disrespectful treatment. Ruthlessness, callousness and arrogance don't belong here."* Apparently neither did legal and ethical behavior.

Amazingly, in researching this section I found sample core values templates, apparently for those enterprises that cannot conjure up their own. That is truly sad, and I can't think of any better reason to look for a new approach to defining purpose. After all, defining your enterprise's purpose just shouldn't be that hard; in fact, I would argue that it should be an organic and enjoyable process.

A Different Approach: Patagonia's Purpose

Having reviewed the pitfalls and pratfalls of mission, vision, and values statements, I'll propose a simpler approach that is perhaps best exemplified by Patagonia, a maker of sporting apparel and equipment that is well known for its environmental focus and adherence to core values. Founder Yvon Chouinard crafted a short mission statement followed by some company history, titled "Our Reason for Being."

First, the mission statement:

> *"Build the best product, cause no unnecessary harm, use business to inspire and implement solutions to the environmental crisis."*

Short, concise, and powerful—a good mission statement. Next, the story of Patagonia's origins, what it values, and why it has been successful.

> *"Patagonia grew out of a small company that made tools for climbers. Alpinism remains at the heart of a worldwide business*

that still makes clothes for climbing—as well as for skiing, snowboarding, surfing, fly fishing, paddling and trail running. These are all silent sports. None requires a motor; none delivers the cheers of a crowd. In each sport, reward comes in the form of hard-won grace and moments of connection between us and nature.

"Our values reflect those of a business started by a band of climbers and surfers, and the minimalist style they promoted. The approach we take towards product design demonstrates a bias for simplicity and utility. For us at Patagonia, a love of wild and beautiful places demands participation in the fight to save them, and to help reverse the steep decline in the overall environmental health of our planet. We donate our time, services and at least 1% of our sales to hundreds of grassroots environmental groups all over the world who work to help reverse the tide.(. . .) Staying true to our core values during thirty-plus years in business has helped us create a company we're proud to run and work for. And our focus on making the best products possible has brought us success in the marketplace."

I like this purpose description for what it says, and more importantly because it is doable and livable, believable, and appealing to potential employees and customers alike. Finally, it is "sticky," in the words of Chip and Dan Heath, authors of *Made to Stick*. It is memorable and the core elements would readily stick in the minds of employees and customers.

Finding Your Own Purpose

By now I hope I've convinced you that 1) having a clear and compelling purpose is essential, and 2) the classic mission, vision, and values statements are not necessarily the best way to express that purpose.

The concerns and considerations behind an organization's purpose can vary at different levels of the organization, so I've broken this section into two parts. The first part is for senior executives who effectively "own" their organization's purpose, and the second is for team leaders or business unit managers who have to create purpose within that larger context.

For CEOs and Executives

Even when executives have a clear sense of purpose, their employees often don't understand and share it. That can be frustrating. Here are a few thoughts about creating a compelling purpose:

- Start from your own roots: what led to your organization's formation?

- Empathize with and understand the points of view of your customers, constituents, and stakeholders, including employees.

- Write from the heart. Contrived and obviously bogus statements are a turnoff.

- Keep it simple. Words don't gain power from number and density, but from simple, thoughtful choices.

- Get buy-in from your reports and employees by including at least some of them in the creation process.

- Test, learn, and be prepared to revise. It's unlikely that your first shot at defining purpose will be spot on. Test it on anybody who will listen and refine it based on feedback. This is a great agile, iterative exercise.

- Create language that won't have to be changed every time business strategy changes.

- Remember that the top-level purpose needs to cascade out to each sub-organization so that when viewed from the bottom up, there is alignment.

Also, give your proposed purpose the "get out of bed test." Simply put, will it inspire you and your employees to get out of bed energized and ready for work? If not, then "rinse and repeat" until you pass this crucial test. The great bluesman Muddy Waters sang, "I love the life I live, and I live the life I love." Your organization's purpose should make you feel that way.

If you are tempted to hand off creation of this document to marketing, or another person who is a better writer or more creative than you think you are—don't. It has to be crafted in your words, since you will repeat them until they are embedded into the organization's DNA. Nothing is more painful than listening to executives or managers parroting words that are clearly not their own and trying to sound passionate. If you enjoy hearing snickers at your all-hands meetings, by all means use a ghostwriter; otherwise, sharpen your pencil. (You can always have an editor give it the once-over.)

Finally, having a common purpose is important—an organization comprised of departments whose purposes and missions don't interconnect is going to be dysfunctional. Imagine a sled dog team with each dog free to head in any direction. The sled wouldn't go anywhere. Each employee needs to realize how her job and the role of her team or department contribute to the broader purpose of the enterprise. Defining purpose is not a project—it's a journey.

For Team Leaders and Business Unit Managers

While the CEO has a blank slate on which to formulate a purpose statement, the same is not true for those in the middle of the organization. As a team lead or manager, you have the challenge of creating a sense of purpose for your team in the context of the larger organization, which may have a lackluster set of mission, vision, and values statements and may be lacking an identifiable purpose. Some thoughts:

- Borrowing from Donella Meadows' *Thinking in Systems* mentioned in Chapter 2, spend some time observing the behaviors of the business or organization to identify its true purpose—not merely the stated mission, vision, and values. That is the context in which your employees will be viewing your organization's purpose.

- If your organization lacks definable purpose—or worse, has a disagreeable one—don't be discouraged. Just follow the remaining steps. It is possible to create an island of purpose in a sea of randomness. You may need to ignore the advice about alignment that I gave your boss in the preceding section, or, better, work to try to convince senior management of the need for compelling organizational purpose.

- Borrowing from lean thinking, identify your customers, whether internal or external, and drill down on how you create value for them. That is an essential part of your purpose and helps connect your team to customers, which is a very good thing.

- Think about what is important to you and your team. What gets the juices flowing and drives superior performance?

- Capture those thoughts and share them with the team, or, in a larger organization, a cross-section of the unit. Gather feedback, redraft, and recirculate until the result feels right.

Living Purpose

When enterprises create mission, vision, and values statements, they generally launch a communications program that includes announcements at all-hands meetings, exhortations to managers to carry the statements to their departments, and a variety of slogan-bearing cards, placards, and the like.

Save yourself time and money—those approaches don't work very well and they certainly don't stick. I can testify from experience that carrying a plastic card inscribed with "our corporate values" does not make those values come to life. I worked at a company where managers were instructed to stop employees randomly and challenge them to recite the corporate mission and values. Energizing? No.

Purpose is to be lived, not just spoken. Think about how concepts and values that are captured in the purpose narrative are, or become, part of the fabric of organizational language and culture. Start with the leadership team: its members should integrate the language into their own communication so it flows naturally and becomes something that is talked about, not just broadcast.

More importantly, the organization's leaders need to live and demonstrate the values continually, not just when convenient. As Giblin and Muso showed, stating core values and then ignoring them when financially expedient is a real downer.

Second, look for opportunities to create stories and organizational "lore" that encapsulate the organization's purpose. I highly recommend that you bring customers to all-hands or team meetings to explain how your organization's products and services improve their quality of life. Hearing from real clients about their experiences can be a strong motivator for everyone in the organization. Think about how much reach the famous Nordstrom tire story has had—evoking a devotion to customer service so strong that an employee would take back a product that wasn't even sold by the store. Powerful stuff, even if its authenticity has been questioned. Now think about one of your customers with a similar (true) story talking to your team.

Finally, use every opportunity to inject the concepts and values contained in the purpose statement into everyday conversation. Getting employees and managers to continually reflect on and use the purpose statement to guide their day-to-day decisions and actions is the ultimate acid test. That is a big step toward an energized enterprise.

Following are suggestions for further reading on meaningful purpose statements before we move on to Chapter 4, on focused leadership.

Resources

- Cardani, Leann. 2000. *Corporate Mission Statements: A Strategic Management Issue.* University of St. Francis.

- Fleming, John, and Dan Witters. July 2012. *Your Employees Don't "Get" Your Brand.* Gallup Business Journal.

- Giblin, Edward, and Linda Amuso. 1997. *Putting Meaning Into Corporate Values*, California State University.

- Heath, Chip, and Dan Heath. 2007. *Made to Stick.* Random House.

- Jackall, Robert. 1988. *Moral Mazes: The World of Corporate Managers.* Oxford University Press.

- Karlgaard, Rich. July 2009. *Purpose-Driven Leadership*, Forbes. com.

- McSween, Daschell. 2010. *Get Inspiration From These 10 Famous Vision Statements*, BrightHub.

CHAPTER 4

FOCUSED LEADERSHIP

"There is surely nothing quite so useless as doing with great efficiency what should not be done."—Peter Drucker

Prime the Engine: Pre-Reading Questions

1. Do you have a formal process for managing priorities?

2. Do actual projects, initiatives, and day-to-day work match stated priorities?

3. Do you have more externally (customer) focused priorities than internally focused?

4. If you asked each level of management, and then employees, what your organization's top five priorities are, would the answers be consistent?

If you answered "no" to any questions, this chapter will help you focus.

Introduction

Focus is a rare commodity today. As I write this chapter, my laptop tries to lure me into checking Facebook, Twitter, or LinkedIn, or perhaps surfing the web to see what's happening outside the four walls of my office. For business leaders the distractions may be different, but they are still potent forces to drag them away from what needs to get done.

Executives have the seemingly impossible task of balancing the needs of customers, employees, and stakeholders while plotting strategy, countering competitors' moves, and navigating turbulent business environments. How can they do that? One word—focus.

The Focus Challenge

Focus: 1) Close or narrow attention; concentration. 2) To direct toward a particular point or purpose. 3) To concentrate attention or energy.

"He has the attention span of a gnat."

"She can't stay focused on anything."

"When everything is a priority, nothing is a priority."

Refrains like these reveal a focus problem. Managers that are "focus-challenged" are driven by the problem *du jour*, or the article they just read, or something a family member said or did. They never met an idea they didn't like, and they can't wait to unleash that cool idea on their employees, who are then expected to embrace and act on it.

I can't think of anything more destructive to morale and productivity than managers with ants in their pants. You know the type. They pop into your cubicle with their latest great idea or—worse-yet—a drop-everything fire drill caused by a critical remark from a single customer or acquaintance.

One complaint, one service issue, one lost sale becomes a tsunami of disastrous portent that requires immediate attention. For managers, it's an adrenaline "I'm in charge" rush. For employees, it's "here we go again" eye rolling and cynicism. The result is chaos and demoralized employees who eventually leave out of frustration with not being able to excel at their jobs.

Lack of focus is problematic, but that raises the question, "focus on what?" Drawing from our lean-thinking tool kit, the short answer is "focus on priorities that create value for customers and leverage what your organization does best." Financial and other performance metrics are important but aren't an end unto themselves. They are merely snapshots of how your organization is or isn't reaping the benefits of providing value to customers.

How Big a Challenge?

I know that focus is a challenge for executives and organizations: I've watched and lived it up close and personal. And a 2011 survey by Booz & Company backs me up. Here are some findings from the survey of 2,800 executives:

- 64% said their biggest frustration factor is "having too many priorities."

- 56% reported challenges in allocating resources in a way that supports their strategy.

- 54% do not feel that their strategy will lead to success.

If executives can't manage priorities and align resources with strategies that actually work, we are all in a world of hurt. Imagine getting on a cruise ship without knowing its destination because the captain has so many choices he can't make up his mind. And, he'll think of new destinations once the cruise gets underway. And, he's not sure if he has enough fuel, food, and supplies to get to any given destination.

It gets better. The same research revealed that companies pursuing fewer priorities perform significantly better than those pursuing many priorities. Fully 44% of firms with 1-3 priorities were rated as performing above industry averages, compared to only 28% of firms with 10 or more priorities. Astoundingly, the 49% of respondents who had *no* list of priorities performed only a percentage point worse than than those pursuing 10 or more.

Figure 7: Priorities Versus Performance

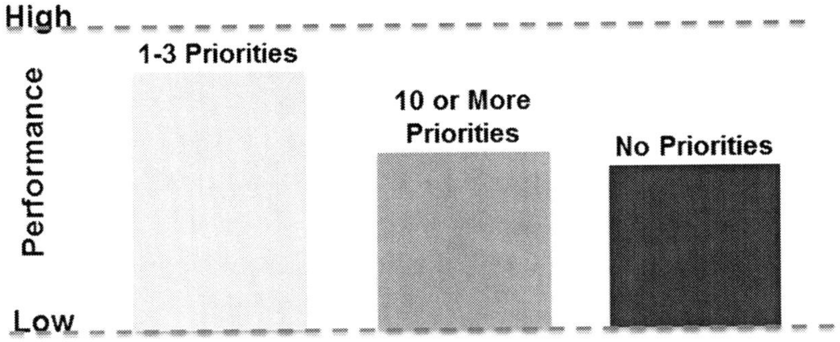

While executives bemoan too many priorities, their organizations are underperforming. Sounds like a big challenge, doesn't it?

The Focus Test

Since those who can't focus may lack the focus to actually realize it, I've created a simple test. Read the following statements and give yourself two points if you agree, zero points if you disagree.

1. It is painful to sit in meetings with my staff and listen to their ideas because I already know some won't work and there are better ways to do others.

2. Any complaint from a customer is cause for immediate remedial action, including determining whose fault the complaint was.

3. My staff often asks me for help in sorting through their priorities.

4. My staff members complain that they have too much to do and not enough time or resources.

5. My staff has reminded me at least once that my list of key initiatives for the organization repeats items from previous years that I've long since forgotten.

6. I don't have a list of key priorities for my organization, as it would be too confining in a world that changes continuously.

Now, add up your points. If you scored four or less, you are pretty focused. If you scored six, you are borderline unfocused. Eight or above marks you as a genuine "Ricochet Rabbit."

Focus doesn't exist in a vacuum; in fact, it ties directly to other chapters in this book. Having a compelling purpose adds focus by providing an anchor for deciding where to direct energy and resources. Ditto for engaged employees—they are focused on their work.

Tackling the Challenge: Focus on Focus

Focus doesn't come naturally for most of us. Focus is a discipline that involves making decisions and managing priorities. In other words, you can't have it all—at least not all at the same time. Modern business life is complicated and full of tasks that seem to be essential. In reality, some of that is illusory, and the ability to separate the wheat from the chaff separates the winners from the losers.

Focused companies and their management know what they do well, what their customers want and need, and what their stakeholders expect. They are able to ignore distractions, yet they realize when they have to deviate from a planned path or strategy. Apple is a focused company. That focus has not only fueled its success but also made it possible to survive the loss of a visionary CEO, Steve Jobs.

In an interview at the 2012 All Things Digital conference, Apple CEO Tim Cook was asked what he learned from Steve Jobs. His answer was, "I learned that focus is key, not just in running a company, but also in your personal life." Throughout the interview, he made it quite clear that Apple's focus remains creating the best products. When asked about his goals for Apple, he says, "I just want to build great products. If we do that, the other things follow." That is focus. And what's important is that it not only provides, as Mr. Cook says, Apple's "North Star," but it leaves enough latitude for Apple to re-invent itself over and over while still maintaining that "best product" focus.

Note that focus doesn't mean lack of change—if anything, focus can lead to even more change. However, that change is "good" because managers are keeping their eyes on the ball and making course corrections when necessary and appropriate. Apple has successfully segued from iPod to iPhone to iPad without losing its focus on creating insanely great products.

A big challenge is balancing internal focus (on the factors of production) and external focus (on consumers of production). Too much internal focus leads to navel gazing and inbred thinking. Too much external focus can lead to failure to invest in and manage people, technology, and processes, causing slow but inevitable decline. Maintaining balance requires constant monitoring and diligence: in other words, focus.

Focus Requires Coherence

If you are certain that your management team understands and has internalized your organization's priorities, have them each list the top five, preferably in order of importance. If the resulting lists are all in sync—congratulations! You are in rarefied territory. If not, you probably suffer from lack of coherence.

Booz & Company defines coherent organizations as those that focus on what they do best in order to create customer value. I take that a step further and add that organizational coherence comes from having a clearly understood purpose, mission, and goals and objectives (priorities) that align from the top of an organization to the bottom.

Coherence is important because without it, focus is impossible, at least in any effective way. If managers and employees have differing views of what needs to get done, they may be focused but at cross-purposes.

Remember my earlier example of a sled dog team with harnesses allowing each dog to run in any direction? Each dog might be focused, but that would be one incoherent dog team.

Over the years, I've witnessed organizations that lack coherence struggle to remember what their current priorities are. "Wait, I thought that got dropped off the list." "Didn't we finish that one?" Or worse, "does anyone remember what that was about?" These are clear warning signs that an enterprise is not energized, and they can be disconcerting or even alarming for employees.

One management challenge in today's business climate is adapting to change without introducing chaos. Having a coherent and aligned set of priorities and goals is a solid starting point for managing change—hazy and ill-defined priorities are not. A big element of maintaining focus is change management, and that requires a solid baseline that remains visible even as priorities change to meet new needs.

The philosopher Santayana once said that those who forget history are doomed to repeat it. He could well have been speaking about modern organizations. I have witnessed organizations with short memories that end up with "new priorities" that are actually retreads of "old priorities" that were never completed, failed, or simply were buried by new priorities.

Focus on Yourself

Leaders in organizations that lack focus need to own up to the fact that they are likely part of the problem and quite possibly *the* problem. Failure to do so will result in a Groundhog Day scenario where priorities keep colliding, things don't get done, performance suffers, and tomorrow looks pretty much like today.

Every communication that a leader makes is loaded: mentioning that something is interesting or seems important inevitably sets off a chain reaction in which employees try to show loyalty and ambition by leaping into action. I've watched teams labor on tasks that were inadvertently set off by managers making an offhand remark. Imagine how demoralizing it is to a team or individual to find out, after working late hours and achieving something difficult, that their leader was merely "thinking out loud."

A manager's job is not to come up with the best ideas. Don Draper of *Mad Men* fame is not a great role model for a manager. Yet, I've known managers who think they are burnishing their image by flinging out a seemingly endless stream of "great ideas." Then they wonder why nothing seems to get done and express frustration with their organization's lack of agility.

In fact, their organizations may be quite agile in jumping through an unceasing assortment of hoops while zigging and zagging to new priorities. Unfortunately, ideas are a dime a dozen, and if the torrent of ideas stymies execution, the ideas are worse than useless.

Every time you get a great new idea, go back to the organizational priority list. If the new idea doesn't dovetail with existing priorities *and* it isn't more important than the existing priorities, park it and forget about it until existing priorities are accomplished.

Focus on Getting the Right Things Done Right

While many businesses have processes for developing annual goals, objectives, plans, and budgets, far fewer seem to have a discipline around managing the priorities that come out of said goals, plans, and budgets. In many cases, plans are adhered to even when it is clear that changing circumstances have rendered them ineffective. Or, the best-laid plans are obliterated by endless fire drills and "new initiatives." What is surprising about the prevalence of focus-challenged organizations is that a lot of tools and techniques exist that can help in managing priorities and maintaining focus.

Systems thinking, lean thinking, and agile thinking, discussed in Chapter 2, are relevant to focus.

- Systems thinking teaches us that changes in any system will likely have an impact on other parts of the system. That means that those hot new initiatives and priorities are loaded with potential for collateral damage.

- Lean thinking teaches us that value springs from a customer's point of view and that we should focus on activities that add value while removing as many others as possible.

- Agile thinking teaches us to use business value to prioritize work, and then to accomplish that work via short, iterative cycles.

One additional tool to add to the kit is called MoSCoW, which is an acronym that represents "must, should, could, and won't" with o's added to make it memorable. MoSCoW, like some of the other practices I've discussed, is drawn from the software world where it is used to prioritize user requirements. It also turns out to be a handy tool for prioritizing business "to-do" lists—simply replace the word "requirement" with "priority" in the following list.

MoSCoW was designed to help developers and business stakeholders develop a common language about requirements. It employs four levels of importance:

1. Must: Requirement that must be satisfied in order to achieve success

2. Should: Requirement that should be included if possible

3. Could: Requirement that is considered desirable but not necessary

4. Won't: Requirement that stakeholders have agreed will not be done

Figure 8 depicts the use of MoSCoW in setting priorities for an agile project.

Figure 8: MoSCoW for Setting Agile Priorities

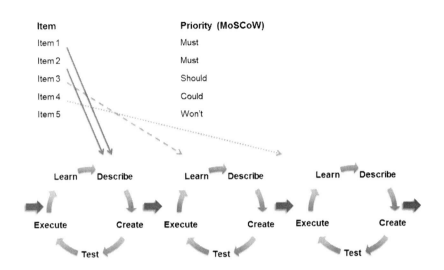

The key to MoSCoW is that it uses plain English to describe priorities in a non-ambiguous way. It is more definitive than the more common "high, medium, and low," priority designations. MoSCoW helps maintain focus when used to create, vet, and manage corporate, departmental, and even individual priority lists. Of course, that presumes that you have priority lists, unlike the 49% of executives described earlier. If not, there's no time like the present to create them.

For CEOs and Executives

Focus has to start at the top—no excuses. The senior management team needs to have the basic discipline to pick a line of attack and stick to it, changing as necessary to meet changing conditions. Without that, chaos will reign. The first order of business in getting an organization focused is to get the management team focused. CEOs and executives should do the following:

- Assess the current level of focus (or lack thereof). A combination of self-reflection and talking to employees who will be candid will usually reveal focus issues quickly. Ensure that most, if not all, priorities are tied to creating customer value *and* based on what the organization does well.

- If you find that your organization is "focus-challenged," the next step is to admit that you (and the management team) are likely a big part of the problem. Most employees don't come to work dreaming of new ways they can spend their day—that is usually directed (or inflicted) by managers.

- Identify and review current priorities to ensure they are relevant, up-to-date, and complete, but not too numerous. Spend the necessary time to remedy any issues and then make sure the vetted priorities are continually communicated across the organization.

- Put disciplines in place, and use tools like MoSCoW to manage priorities.

- Deputize objective "bystanders" to report straying from objectives. Find a person or people who will stand up to managers or teams and say "wait, that's not on our priority list—why are we doing that?"

The old saw that "the buck stops here" really applies to organizational focus. I've never seen a focused, disciplined company with unfocused, undisciplined management, and I doubt that such a company exists.

For Team Leaders and Business Unit Managers

While working for a senior executive who lacks focus and discipline is trying, that is no excuse for giving up. Your employees expect and deserve help in managing their priorities, which means you have to come to grips with managing yours and those of your organization. Here's how:

- Assess your current priorities and their alignment to those of the larger organization. As you move further down in a large organization, departmental or group priorities may be less tightly tied to creating customer value, but there should be at least some linkage.

- Borrow a practice from IT organizations and start tracking "change requests"—requests or directions from managers to shift resources or, worse yet, priorities without resources. Keep a running tally and make it part of your process of measuring organizational effectiveness. What isn't measured can't be managed, and what isn't documented doesn't get fixed.

- The best defense is a good offense—keep a tight list of highly visible priorities that can be used to fend off rogue priority requests from other organizations. Train your staff in the gentle art of persuasion in using that list.

- Develop a simple process for vetting new priorities, whether they originate within or outside of your organization. Compare new priorities to existing ones and make adjustments (hopefully sparingly) where necessary.

Focus is core and key to organizational performance. We've seen that executives are stymied by too many priorities; organizations also suffer from lack of focus, yet it remains a prevalent problem. Think globally about focus, and then act locally where you can have impact.

Living Focused

While focus is a discipline that can be difficult to instill and maintain, it is also tremendously liberating. Just like cleaning old junk out of the garage so the car once again fits, clearing out the detritus of has-been priorities can bring energy to an organization. In short, focus is a key ingredient to an energized enterprise. It is also a key tool in engaging staff and employees, covered in Chapter 5.

Following are resources used for this chapter and suggestions for additional reading on this topic.

Resources

- Allen, Frederick. 2012. *Study Finds That Having Power Can Make You Stupid*, Forbes Magazine.

- Booz & Company. 2011. *Coherence Profiler: Summary of Results.* Booz & Company

- Haughey, Duncan PMP. *MoSCoW Method*, ProjectSmart. co.uk.

- Leinwand, Paul, and Cesare Mainardi, 2011. *Stop Chasing Too Many Priorities.* Harvard Business Review.

- Leinwand, Paul, and Cesare Mainardi. 2010. *The Coherence Premium.* Harvard Business Review.

- Spann, David. 2009. *Secret to Becoming a Lean/Agile Enterprise: Leaders Acting Well Together.* BPM Institute.

- The Economist Technology Quarterly. March 3, 2012. *Taking the Long View.*

- Townsend, Maya. 2012. *Managing Your Organization's Priorities.* Corporate Education Group.

CHAPTER 5

ENGAGED EMPLOYEES

"Devising and maintaining an atmosphere in which others can put a dent in the universe is the leader's creative act."—Warren Bennis

"When the sage's work is done, the people will say, 'we did it ourselves.'"—Lao Tzu

Prime the Engine: Pre-Reading Questions

1. Do your employees wake up in the morning eager to take on the challenges and opportunities of their workday? Do you?

2. Are employees focused on results and outcomes or simply scratching items off their to-do lists?

3. Do employees trust the senior management team?

4. Do your employees have autonomy to decide how, where, and when they will do their work?

In an energized enterprise, the answers would be 1) yes, 2) focused on results and outcomes, 3) yes, and 4) yes. If that's not your case, let this chapter engage you.

Introduction

Employee engagement is one of the key engines of energized enterprises. After all, employees do the work that keeps your enterprise in business. If they are running on empty, performance will be lackluster. The bad news is that surveys conducted by Gallup, Inc. have found 71% of workers disengaged or actively disengaged in their work, resulting in $300 billion in lost productivity. Think about it: fewer than one in three employees (29%) are engaged.

Those are disturbing statistics, and a big problem for organizations and their employees. Getting employees engaged in their work isn't rocket science, but it does take thought and effort. The good news is that companies with engaged employees significantly outperform those without them, as we'll see in this chapter. The first step is examining the difference between motivation and engagement and why that difference matters.

Why Engagement and Not Motivation?

While engagement and motivation are sometimes used interchangeably, they aren't the same thing. Clinical Psychologist Dr. Paul Marciano, in his blog, Whiteboard, distinguishes between the two as follows: "Engagement refers to an intrinsic, deep-rooted, and sweeping sense of commitment, pride, and loyalty that is not easily altered. In contrast, one's level of motivation is strongly influenced by external factors, especially expectations that certain efforts or accomplishments will yield valued rewards, such as a financial bonus for meeting a quarterly sales objective."

There are a lot of definitions of employee engagement. Many focus on the employee's involvement in her company and/or work, but I think that the definition should include reference to outcomes, specifically an employee's involvement in ensuring the furthering of her organization's interests. According to Scarlett Surveys, "Employee engagement is a measurable degree of an employee's positive or negative emotional attachment to their job, colleagues and organization which profoundly influences their willingness to learn and perform at work."

This chapter focuses on engagement and not motivation because engagement is by far the more powerful of the two, albeit more difficult to attain.

Highly engaged employees are more likely to remain motivated even when adverse circumstances such as inadequate job resources, difficult customers, or time pressures make their jobs hard. Motivation alone, on the other hand, can thrive during "good times" but evaporate when the going gets tough. It is critical to understand which one you are trying to achieve, and my vote goes to engagement.

Why Does Employee Engagement Matter?

Why do you care about engagement? After all, you pay your employees and they come to work and do their jobs—isn't that good enough?

Not if you want to be a high-performing organization. A 2010 study by Hewitt Associates found that high-engagement firms had total shareholder return 19% higher than average in 2009, while low-engagement organizations exhibited total shareholder return 44% below average. Gallup, Inc. has found that companies with "world class engagement" have 3.9 times the earnings per share (EPS) growth rate when compared with lower engagement peers. In short, high-engagement organizations outperform their low-engagement peers.

Another reason you should care about engagement is "Bill Joy's Law," coined by Bill Joy, co-founder of Sun Microsystems, which states that, "no matter who you are, most of the smart people work for someone else." If your employees are not engaged, then *all* of the smart people work for someone else.

And then there are the younger members of the workforce that Fast Company has dubbed "Generation Flux." They have some radical, newfangled ideas that their work should be meaningful, they should be working on important initiatives, and they should get frequent feedback on their performance. In other words, they not only want but also expect to be engaged employees, or they will follow Bill Joy's Law right out the door.

Unfortunately, the odds are that your employees are not engaged.

Exhibit One:

- Trust in senior management has a stronger correlation with higher engagement than trust in immediate managers, but only 52% of North American workers trust their executives. (BlessingWhite, 2011)

- Only 33% of employees agreed with the statement, "I will be an important part of this organization in the future." (Gallup, Inc., 2009)

- Only 41% of employees agreed that their executive management had "created a work environment that drives high performance." (BlessingWhite, 2011)

Exhibit Two: When you are out and about, listen to comments from employees of other businesses. Airports are a great place to research employee disengagement—just listen to conversations and mobile phone calls around you. I do, and it is a fascinating peek into the lives and frustrations of employees and managers of organizations of all types. It is an encyclopedia of the ways that employees get disengaged from their companies and their work. There are a lot of unhappy employees out there. (I don't eavesdrop, by the way, people simply talk too loudly.)

Early in my managerial career, when employees complained about their jobs, my reply was essentially "if it were fun, they wouldn't have to pay us." Fortunately, I figured out pretty quickly that this answer wasn't helpful and didn't spur engagement. I also learned a lesson that many organizations still haven't—engaged employees are more productive than disengaged ones, and better yet, more fun to work with. When I quit being snarky and focused on engagement, the results were positively dramatic.

How Management Disengages Employees

One trick I use in figuring out how to make something happen is to examine why it isn't already happening. A good way to start determining how to engage people is to understand what disengages them from their work in the first place. I can come up with three fundamental reasons why your employees would be disengaged:

- You systematically hire disengaged people.

- The work your organization does and/or its mission is so deadly dull it would disengage anybody.

- Something about the management or culture of the organization is causing employees to be disengaged.

If you are hiring disengaged people, stop. They are likely to focus on what's in it for them, not what value they can bring to your organization. If you have tagged the work or mission of your organization as the culprit, unfortunately I have to disagree. Maintaining reasonable working conditions, hiring people who are at a level to be challenged by the work (there are people who fit in even tedious jobs), and recognizing their successes can go a long way to create engagement. That leaves only one reason, the focus of this chapter: management and culture.

There are many examples of how management and culture can disengage employees. It turns out that the road to engagement starts with stopping certain behaviors. The following list contains management behaviors I have directly observed and/or been subject to, and I can attest to their engagement-sapping power:

- Lobbing lots of "great ideas" at already overworked staff. This becomes even more dispiriting if they are ideas that staff already thought of but can't act on because of their workload.

- Giving feedback on performance only during annual appraisals. The shock and awe of a bad review for an employee who has not received feedback on their work for a year is powerful.

- Providing no context or explanation when requesting an employee to do something. More disengagement occurs when the role and assignments don't in any way leverage the employee's skills or interests.

- Making employees repeatedly explain what they do and having them track how they spend their time when they ask for resources or speak up about feeling overloaded. This becomes completely disengaging when no action is taken on the information.

- Monitoring employee behaviors both online and off. Forbidding telecommuting because "if employees can't be trusted to stay focused at work, then they can be trusted even less at home."

- Taking it out on your team after your boss scolds you for poor performance.

- Deploying the infamous "bi-directional I." When things are going well, using "I" a lot to make sure your boss knows how great you are. However, when your boss chews you up and spits you out, using "I" in the martyr sense to gain sympathy.

- Not dealing with underperforming managers. Worse yet, having HR tell employees that such managers are really their own problem and they should handle it by "managing upward."

- Gathering the troops to proclaim that "we" have a serious issue, and then doing nothing to fix it.

- Using raises and promotions to replace genuine support and appreciation of your employees.

- Getting creative in announcing poor financial and performance results to keep morale from deteriorating. For example, saying it's a "timing issue" when expenses exceed sales, rather than the more forthright revenue shortfall or miss. Warning—people catch on to this type of thing quickly.

I wish I could say that this list was invented, but it isn't—I've witnessed or lived all of these. In fact, I could have easily doubled or tripled this list. I can personally attest to the negative impact of managers and organizations that disengage employees.

Engagement vs. Motivation: The Difference Matters

Now that I've explained the rudiments of actions that disengage employees, I'll take a more positive approach and look at ways to engage them.

Knowingly or not, many organizations focus on employee motivation in hope of achieving engagement. They generally use financial rewards such as bonuses and raises. Unfortunately, those rewards may exert some influence on motivation but not on engagement—in fact they may lower engagement.

Daniel Pink's book *Drive* contains good ideas for understanding how to motivate and engage people. Pink unveils research showing that contingent rewards (do this and you'll get that) not only don't work but actually negatively affect people doing work that is, or should be, intrinsically motivating and engaging. He argues that extrinsic perks and bonuses are less effective in gaining employee engagement when work is intrinsically motivating than when it isn't.

How does one make work intrinsically motivating and engaging? By moving from empowerment to autonomy and mastery as a focus in managing people. Empowerment has been the Holy Grail of talent management for many years, but it's only a step on the path to full engagement.

Instead of empowerment, Pink favors autonomy, mastery, and purpose. When all three come together, the result is "flow," a state of engagement described by Mihaly Csikszentmihalyi based on research conducted at the University of Chicago. Flow is an amazing phenomenon where time, place, and self virtually disappear because you are so engaged in what you are doing. Flow is the Holy Grail of engagement. I'll focus here on autonomy and mastery since Chapter 2 is devoted to purpose. (To recap briefly, the main takeaway from Chapter 2 is that a clear and compelling purpose is a key ingredient to driving performance and energy in organizations.)

Autonomy involves giving employees the freedom to be self-directed in their work. Not "empowered" to do what they are told, but free to determine how, when, and where they do the work that needs to be done. Pink is careful to note that autonomous workers still have goals and are still held accountable for their work, but that performance is judged based on results: what they do, and how well it's done.

Mastery is simply getting better at doing something that matters. Pink refers to three laws of mastery:

1. Mastery is Pain: it will require hard work and determination.

2. Mastery is a Mindset: it requires a mindset that abilities can be enhanced and improved through work.

3. Mastery is an Asymptote: total achievement will never be attained, but one can get closer and closer to that goal.

The notion of mastery makes clear that there are two sides to engagement. Employees have to bring to the table energy and determination, while managers have to ensure that work is matched to employees' skills and interests.

The Road to Engagement

Flow, autonomy, mastery, and purpose are all nice concepts, but what do they look like in practice? The immediate temptation is to devise some programmatic way to make them happen. Better yet, assign it to HR—that sounds like something they should do! But the reason many managers struggle to engage employees is that they seek one-size-fits-all solutions. Employees are individuals and most want to be treated and seen that way. That means managers have to work harder to figure out how to engage them, and it means HR, while able to provide support, can't make this happen alone.

That said, I do believe some basic components would be near universally important to engagement. Employees should:

- Work for an organization whose mission or purpose makes their work feel important

- Know what's expected of them and have adequate resources to do their work

- Have associates that are committed to doing quality work

- Be treated as individuals, with respect and dignity

- Have the opportunity to do work that is challenging and requires learning and growth, but not beyond their capabilities

- Have the freedom to decide how, when, and where to perform their work. (Yes, there are cases where freedom has to be limited—I don't want my surgery done at the surgeon's home, and a receptionist has to sit at an office's front desk—but it is usually possible to find some aspects of work that are suitable for more autonomy.)

- Be accountable for achieving goals and results

- Receive feedback as well as recognition for work well done on a regular basis

- Like and respect direct managers and the senior management team

That isn't a complete list, but I believe that any workplace exhibiting those characteristics would drive positive employee engagement and performance. Now the challenge is to create such an organization. The following section contains advice for executives and managers on how to improve employee engagement on the road to an energized enterprise.

For CEOs and Executives

I believe that engagement should be the No. 1 concern of any CEO or executive because the negative effects of disengaged employees are so damaging. The BlessingWhite survey cited earlier found that executives have a stronger impact on employee engagement than the employees' direct management, yet only slightly more than half of surveyed workers actually trust their executives, and less than half feel that executives create an environment conducive to high performance levels. Here are some suggested actions:

- Assess the current level of engagement by asking and listening to all levels of the organization. Don't ask, "Are you engaged?" Instead, focus on the factors that promote or inhibit engagement, such as challenging work, adequate resources, recognition, and so forth.

- Only conduct engagement surveys if you plan to act on them. Failure to implement visible changes may actually decrease engagement.

- If engagement is lacking, focus on the inhibitors. Use systems thinking, because lack of engagement is not a "point problem" and won't lend itself to point solutions. Start by looking in the mirror since management practices are a common and powerful engagement inhibitor.

- Identify your own roots of disengagement (and those of your management team). If you are not engaged in your executive role, figure out why and fix it.

- Be patient—this is one of the most difficult aspects of creating an energized enterprise.

The key advice in this section is to take a systemic view of, and approach to, employee engagement. It's tempting to leap on solving immediately visible disengaging factors, but the reality is, they don't exist in isolation. Tease disengagement apart to find all the key elements, remedy them, and then focus on improving engagement.

For Team Leaders and Business Unit Managers

Your first step is to look in the mirror and assess your level of engagement. If you are not engaged, it is unlikely that your employees will be. Manager, heal thyself. Here are some thoughts for you:

- If you are not engaged, figure out why and tackle it head on.

- If disengagement is a problem, determine its origin. Excessive administrivia is an easy place to start as endless paperwork, meetings, and such are a real drain on energy and enthusiasm. It's difficult to engage with your work when you have to keep tending to other things that are not in any way engaging.

- Engage your employees in getting engaged. Talk about the engaging and disengaging aspects of their work, and have them help tweak roles and assignments to make work more engaging.

- If senior management is sucking the life out of your organization through some of the behaviors noted earlier, tackle them head on if at all possible. (The behaviors. Not senior managers.)

- Do not try to solve engagement issues strictly with monetary rewards. Yes, monetary compensation is important, but it won't solve deep-rooted underlying engagement issues. Resolve to tackle the real needs and issues.

As a manager or leader, you are the front line in engaging employees. Even though the BlessingWhite data shows that executives have a stronger impact on engagement than direct managers, many of the variables that drive or inhibit engagement are also found at the direct management level.

Living Engagement

Hopefully by now I've convinced you that engaged employees are not just a hallmark of energized enterprises; they're a foundational element. Achieving engagement is not an exercise or an initiative. It's a journey that never ends. And it's not easy—just as mastery requires perseverance and work, so does engagement. I liken it to building organizational muscle.

However, the rewards for that hard work are significant, as the performance statistics cited in this chapter attest. What those statistics don't fully show is how much more enjoyable it is to work in an organization with engaged managers and employees. And that is likely to positively affect customer relations, the topic of Chapter 6.

Resources

- Blacksmith, Nikki, and Jim Harter. 2011. *Majority of American Workers Not Engaged in Their Jobs*. Gallup, Inc.

- Gallup Consulting. 2010. *State of the American Workplace: 2008-2010*. Gallup, Inc.

- Haid, Michael, and Jamie Sims. 2009. *Employee Engagement, Maximizing Organizational Performance*. Right Management.

- Kamenetz, Anya. February 2012. *Generation Flux*. Wired Magazine.

- Marciano, Paul, Ph.D. 2009. *Employee Engagement vs. Motivation*. Whiteboard.

- Pink, Daniel. 2006. *Drive: The Surprising Truth About What Motivates Us*. Penguin Books.

- Rice, Christopher. 2011. *Employee Engagement Report 2011. Beyond the Numbers*. BlessingWhite.

- Sanborn, Pete, Rahul Malhotra, and Amy Atchinson. 2011. *Trends in Global Employee Engagement*. AonHewitt.

CHAPTER 6

CUSTOMER INTIMACY

"The single most important thing to remember about any enterprise is that there are no results inside its walls. The result of a business is a satisfied customer."—Peter Drucker

Prime the Engine: Pre-Reading Questions

1. Do all of your employees (not just managers) know who your customers are and why they buy your products and services?

2. Does your management team frequently meet with customers on their own turf?

3. Do all employees (not just sales and marketing) consider customers as their responsibility?

4. When your team meets with customers, who does most of the talking?

Your first three answers should be "yes," and your last one "customers." If not, read on.

Introduction

Customer intimacy does not mean getting into bed with your customers, at least not literally. It also is not only about customer relationship management (CRM), social CRM, social media, voice of the customer, engagement, customer experience management, or any of the other plethora of marketing terms that purport to put the customer "first." (Although it does encompass those.) Nor is it the confluence of big data and analytics which enables companies to micro-target customers based on demographics, purchase histories, and web-surfing behaviors.

Customer intimacy is a business model that focuses on creating trusted relationships with customers and delivering heightened value to them based on that connection. It is a two-way street, with companies and customers engaged in a mutually beneficial relationship. It is also important for creating energized enterprises, as customers are a key catalyst in energizing an enterprise.

I chose "intimacy" over "focus" for this chapter's theme as many enterprises are focused on customers—or, more accurately, their wallets—but seem to have no interest in a deeper relationship in which monetary and non-monetary value flows from customer to business and business to customer. I also chose "intimacy" over "customer service" as I believe that customer relationships need to be deeper than just providing superior customer service (although that is a great place to start).

Organizations that embrace customer intimacy treat customers as peers and equals and strive for an exchange of trust and value based on mutual respect. Is that a tall order? Yes it is, but it's also totally achievable. This chapter aims to help you understand customer intimacy and convince you to embark on that journey.

What is Customer Intimacy?

> *Customer: A person who buys, esp. on a regular basis.*
> *Intimacy: Characterized by very close association or familiarity.*

Most consumers feel businesses can do more to retain their loyalty, according to the 2010 American Express Global Customer Service Barometer research study. The study revealed that 48% of consumers feel companies are helpful but don't do anything extra to keep their business, and 21% believe that companies take their business for granted. Apparently many enterprises are not hewing to the definitions of customer intimacy.

Most organizations at least mention how much they value customers in their mission and values statements, but apparently many are not actually living those values. In researching this chapter, it was obvious that a small list of companies land on top-10 customer service lists every year, including Apple, Southwest Airlines, and Nordstrom. That would seem to point not only to the challenges in achieving customer intimacy, but also the potential for those that do to rise above the herd.

The earliest mention of customer intimacy I found was in a 1992 Harvard Business Review article written by Michael Treacy, president of Treacy & Company, and Fred Wiersema, vice president of CSC Index. In that article they defined customer intimacy as one of three value disciplines that companies could pursue to achieve dominance in their markets (the other two being product leadership and operational excellence). They defined customer intimacy as "segmenting and targeting markets narrowly and then tailoring offerings to match the demands of those niches."

A lot has happened since 1992, not the least of which is the advent of the web and social media, and a more current definition of customer intimacy—my definition—is somewhat broader. I define it as a mutually beneficial relationship between an enterprise's employees and managers, and its customers, that includes:

- Conversation and listening

- Mutual learning and exchange of valuable information

- Contextual tailoring of information, products, and services to meet individual client needs

- Co-innovation and co-creation of products and services

- Crowd-sourcing for idea generation and support

- Evangelism and promotion

The big difference between my definition and theirs is the notion of bi-directionality and "flatness." Their definition focuses on providing more value to customers by understanding their needs, while mine adds the dimension of receiving value from customers by tapping their innovation and energy. In other words, value flows both ways and is not strictly exchanged for money.

The web has flattened previously hierarchical relationships and gives customers a voice to render opinions on organizations and their offerings. The result is a massive shift in power that can be humbling to companies that haven't fully figured that out yet, and it's a key reason that customer intimacy is so important.

Witness McDonald's and its ill-fated #McDStories Twitter escapade. Customers were asked to tweet about their experiences at McDonald's, and even a casual Twitter user can guess how that worked out. (Hint: more bad than good.) Or how about Qantas, which tempted followers with Qantas gift packs if they would describe their "dream luxury in-flight experience" on Twitter. In response, sarcastic tweets made fun of the airline's ongoing labor dispute with its employees—a marketer's worst nightmare.

In both cases, the companies clearly did not understand that a sizable chunk of their customers were only too happy to share (or even make up) horror stories. That is a failure of customer intimacy at two levels: first, knowing your customers, and second, maintaining positive relationships with them. Venturing into the social media landscape missing either or both of these is like attempting the Running of the Bulls while blindfolded. It will be a heady experience, but it probably won't end well.

On a more positive note, one company that has focused on customer intimacy is Intuit. It has created an approach to product development that involves customers early in the process and also engages them to provide support to other customers. CEO Scott Cook explained in a published interview, "Such a [user contribution] system creates value for a business as a consequence of the value it delivers to users—personalized purchase recommendations, connections between buyers and sellers of hard-to-find items, new personal or business relationships, lower prices, membership in a community, entertainment, information of all kinds."

Back to the Future: The Roots of Customer Intimacy

While it is tempting to view customer intimacy as something new, in reality it is rooted in timeworn behaviors, just manifested in different ways via the Internet. Let's take a deeper look at the tenets of customer intimacy:

- Communications with customers have moved from one-way push marketing to conversations, with customers firmly in control.

- Customers are talking about businesses and products with or without the participation of businesses, and businesses need to earn the right to participate by providing objective and unbiased information.

- Customers expect businesses to deliver superior experiences— not just products and services—the way that they want them, at all stages of the customer life-cycle.

- Value is defined by the customer, and businesses have to ferret out what value means to each customer.

- Some customers have ideas to improve businesses and products and want to share them if businesses will listen *and* act on them.

- Customers who like an organization and its products and services will talk favorably about them.

- Trust is at the foundation of great customer relationships, and trust is difficult to earn but easy to lose.

What's interesting is that many of the elements have actually been around for years. People used to discuss favorite brands and products by the office water cooler—now they do it via Facebook and Twitter. The difference is that the scale and reach of the Internet, coupled with global and diverse populations, has changed how these things happen. Instead of small groups around the water cooler, businesses now are dealing with many customers, potentially scattered around the globe, talking about them 24x7.

If you live in a small town, as I do, you have a tiny window into the past, when customer intimacy was ingrained in the way many shopkeepers ran their businesses. Many of our local businesses are small "mom and pop" stores with proprietors who talk with their customers, listen to feedback, try to provide engaging experiences, work to earn and keep trust, and take advice on how they can improve their businesses. These are the good ones that get my repeat business. For example, I frequent a family-owned music store where a manager not only knows my taste in guitars but also contacts me whenever something "cool" arrives. Result: I have a rather large collection of musical gear and the store has a very loyal customer.

What has changed (outside of small towns, at least) is that the scale of enterprises has made the close, face-to-face relationships that proprietors of yore enjoyed with their customers difficult or impossible. Businesses have struggled to adapt to the rise of the global, 24x7, socially enabled customer, with some successes and some notable failures including those highlighted above.

So, I would argue that customer intimacy is a sort of "back to the future" where organizations of all sizes work to build relationships with customers in an attempt to erase time and distance and to re-establish the types of relationships that existed in that small-town past.

Why Customer Intimacy Matters

While there are many reasons why achieving customer intimacy is important, I'll provide two examples here: first, the struggle by J.C. Penney's new CEO to find a profitable business strategy; second, the precipitous decline of Research In Motion's (RIM) product sales to enterprises.

I believe that former Apple CEO Ron Johnson, upon taking the reins at J.C. Penney, Inc., was acting in what he thought was the customers' interest when he moved from a seemingly confusing mish-mash of promotions and sales to an "everyday low price" strategy. Unfortunately, J.C. Penney's customers seem to prefer "confusing" sales and promotions, as customers defected right after the new pricing schemes were implemented and the store chain took a financial hit. Lesson learned: don't guess about what customers want—ask them.

The second lesson is that what customers value can change, sometimes rapidly. RIM, with its BlackBerry, had the enterprise smartphone market in its pocket based on superior enterprise support that attracted IT organizations. It did not count on the iPhone becoming such a compelling force that iPhone users literally stormed the gates of IT departments demanding to use their own phones—the advent of bring your own device (BYOD). Lesson learned: don't just ask customers once—keep asking, as their answers will change. An ancillary lesson is to make sure you're listening to the right customers. RIM's original customers were IT guys who were late to the BYOD party. RIM really needed to listen to end-user buyers, as they took matters into their own hands and bought the iPhones they really wanted.

Building Blocks for Customer Intimacy

If your first impulse is to just tell employees to mimic those small-store proprietors described earlier, don't, unless you have a small enterprise or you happen to like chaos. That folksy, friendly approach that works so well in a mom-and-pop shop doesn't translate well to a larger enterprise.

Instead, build a road map for the journey to customer intimacy including the following building blocks:

Goals: Start with a firm set of goals and objectives. Know what you are trying to achieve and why. Hint: more sales is probably in there somewhere, but hopefully isn't your singular goal. If it is, customers are likely to figure that out quickly and any notion of intimacy flies out the window. Better goals would include finding out what customers value (or don't value) in your products, what they think about your pricing, and what products you don't offer that they would like.

Value: Borrowing from lean thinking, know what value you can deliver to customers above and beyond products and services. A 2011 IBM study, *From Social Media to Social CRM*, showed deep disconnects between what businesses believe buyers want and what buyers actually reported that they want. In the report, businesses rated discounts and purchasing at the bottom of their lists of reasons why consumers would use social media, while customers put both at the top of their lists. You need to understand what customers want and value before you can develop a meaningful relationship.

Metrics: Once you have nailed what customers really want, it is important to have ways to measure success. Standard metrics include customer retention, upselling, and market share, but newer metrics, especially the concept of net promoter scores, are important as well. A net promoter score is the difference between customers' positive and negative mentions of a company or product—the higher the better.

Customer relationship management: When you are really conversing with customers, you'll be amazed at how much content is generated. That content needs to live somewhere, as it is the basis for developing a deep understanding of customer wants, needs, and behaviors. CRM systems that can manage all of the information about interactions with customers, including external social media sites, are a necessity, as is the organizational discipline to actually use the information.

Social presence: According to the Pew Foundation, 66% of American adults use social media platforms such as Facebook, Twitter, MySpace, and LinkedIn. In a 2011 study, GroupM, a media investment management firm, found that 48% of consumers combine social media and search engines in their buying process. You probably should be on those platforms as well, focused on learning about what customers think, say, and value.

Rules of engagement: While socializing comes naturally to many people, socializing in a business context is somewhat trickier and more error prone. Do not, repeat, do not outsource social media or turn it over to summer interns. Do provide straightforward guidelines and instruction for employees about working with customers.

Especially, focus on giving examples of what great customer engagement looks like, as some employees may have never seen it. On the rare occasions I shop at Macy's, I often wonder why their management doesn't send new hires across the mall to Nordstrom to witness what good customer service looks like. Role models, even from competitors, can be a simple way to help instill customer engagement skills.

Navigating the Customer Intimacy Continuum

Customer intimacy isn't an end point—it is a continuum, where mutual value increases as an organization moves from the left to the right as shown in Figure 9.

Figure 9: From Buyers to Co-Creators

Buyers	Fans	Evangelists	Co-Creators
• Buy products • Use customer service • Provide profitable revenue	• "Like" company • Follow announcements • Share and redistribute announcements	• Promote company, products, and services • Provide personal examples of product value • Provide help to other customers	• Provide feedback on products and services • Co-design and refine products and services • Contribute code, content, or intellectual property

I could argue that customer intimacy is "just good business." After all, which would you rather do business with: an aloof, standoffish company that doesn't seem all that eager to do business with you, or one that anticipates your wants and needs and cares about you beyond being just a revenue source? But there's more—much more. Here are some key reasons why you should be seeking to move from the left to the right in Figure 9:

Buyers: Even if your only interest in customers is their wallets, customer intimacy has a payoff. Jonathan Byrnes, in his 2010 book *Islands of Profit in a Sea of Red Ink*, notes that "every company I have seen is 30%-40% unprofitable by any measure, while 20%-30% provides all of the reported earnings." He goes on to say that the reason is that companies serve all their customers in the same way, failing to understand which customers provide sustained profitability. Byrnes cites Pepsi, Chiquita, and P&G as companies that have used customer intimacy to create profitability even in the depths of a recession.

Going a bit further, customers that like and trust your company are likely to spend more money. According to American Express, Americans will spend 9% more with companies that provide excellent customer service. You can take that to the bank.

Fans: Since I dinged McDonald's earlier for a social media gaffe, it's only fair that I acknowledge a success. In 2010, McDonald's re-launched the McRib sandwich at some locations. They quickly discovered McRib super fans, including one who built a Facebook page dedicated to the sandwich and another who created a Google map where fans could put pins on McDonald's locations that served the McRib. McDonald's used their stories to build buzz on Facebook and Twitter and featured them at a media launch event. The net result was a bunch of new customers and a successful product launch.

Evangelists: The next step beyond fans is evangelism—people who will enthusiastically promote your company, products, and services. These are people who are like virtual employees and spend significant time and energy promoting awareness and goodwill. Who is more believable in talking about a product—the company's sales and marketing folks or a customer that bought the product and likes it? An extreme example is that of Southwest Airlines. In the post-9/11 air travel downturn, its customers not only used social media sites to help persuade others to fly Southwest, but some even donated money to keep it afloat.

Another manifestation of evangelism is support communities where customers help each other with technical or other support issues. Dell, Caterpillar, Salesforce.com, and Microsoft are just a few examples of enterprises that have thriving customer support communities.

Co-Creators: Also known as co-innovators, some customers can come up with product ideas you never would have thought of. Lego, BMW, and Starbucks have all become masters in working with customers to co-create products and services.

Lego, the Danish toy company, has a site called Lego Cuusoo, where enthusiasts can submit and vote on product ideas. One submission, a Lego set based on the Minecraft video game, received 10,000 votes within 24 hours and was given the go-ahead within one month. Lego CEO Jorgen Vig Knudstorp believes that customers are more than mere consumers; they are co-creators with a vested interest in the company's success in creating the products they want. Note that the process is interactive and based on actionable feedback, not survey results that can be difficult to interpret and use.

Co-creators are the top of the top of customer intimacy—imagine the loyalty and resiliency of Lego's customer base. They are highly unlikely to defect to any upstart copycat toymakers.

For CEOs and Executives

Creating and maintaining an organization that lives and breathes customer intimacy is a never-ending job—but it's also fulfilling and energizing. While the lure of using technology to gain a deeper understanding of customers is strong, it isn't a substitute for the spadework that creates an organization with strong and deep relationships with its customers. Here are some key actions:

- Ensure that customer intimacy is a top priority throughout your organization. It needs to be baked into the organization's DNA and lived by all. Don't just talk about it—go visit customers frequently and be highly visible about valuing and using their input.

- Make it possible for employees at all levels of the organization to meet and get to know customers. Trust those who interact with customers and give them the autonomy and tools to meet customers' needs.

- Hire people with great customer skills and get rid of employees without them if their behaviors can't be modified. An amazing number of positive interactions can be undone by one unfavorable one.

- Make it easy for customers to contact anyone in your organization by whatever means they wish. Interactive voice response (IVR) "gauntlets" are a dead giveaway that you don't like talking with customers. Also, ensure that all channels are consistent in policies and messaging.

- Whenever possible, involve customers in product strategy and development—not as a sole source of information and inspiration, but as a critical one.

While customer intimacy is everyone's job, you have the job of setting the tone.

For Team Leaders and Business Unit Managers

If you are a leader or manager of a business unit or team that works directly with customers, your action items look quite similar to those for executives. If your team is somewhat removed from customer contact, you still need to get your staff steeped in customer intimacy. Here are some key actions:

- Find ways to get your staff together with customers—invite customers to staff meetings, encourage senior management to hold open houses, or find opportunities for staff to visit customers. They'll learn things that will enable them to deliver higher levels of service.

- Remind your team that customers are their *raison d'etre*. Yes, customers can present challenges to service and support staff, but without customers there are no requests for help, and ultimately no jobs—it's that simple.

- Engage in storytelling. Find examples of inspiring customer interactions and successes that help staff understand how their work relates to making customers (and your organization) successful.

- Find ways to get your staff to work with customers to solve their specific problems.

Living Customer Intimacy

Imagine an organization that turns itself inside-out to make employees visible and available to prospects and customers. Much time and energy is devoted to understanding each customer's view of value, using not only data mining and analysis but also social media and front-line contact between managers and employees and customers. The organization views its products and services as valuable to customers and treats them accordingly—they aren't "sold" but rather adopted by customers who view them as part of a continuum of value received from the organization.

Service and support are considered part of that value, not cost centers. Customers work with marketing and product development teams to co-create new and better products and services. Customers happily recommend the organization to friends and family because they have such a high level of trust in the organization, its management, and its employees. That is living customer intimacy at an energized enterprise.

And as Chapter 7 shows, it's an essential part of a dynamic company culture.

Resources

- Baird, Carolyn, and Gautam Parasnis. 2011. *From Social Media to Social CRM*. IBM Corporation.

- Barnes, Brooks. 2012. *In Customer Service Consulting, Disney's Small World is Growing*. The New York Times.

- Byrnes, Jonathan. 2011. *Customer Intimacy vs. Operations Excellence: Why Not Have Both?* April 8, Fast Company.

- Byrnes, Jonathan. 2010. *Islands of Profit in a Sea of Red Ink: Why 40 Percent of Your Business Is Unprofitable and How to Fix It*. Portfolio Hardcover.

- McMann & Ransford. 2011. *The Quest for Customer Intimacy*.

- Tracy, Michael, and Fred Wiersema. 1992. *Customer Intimacy and Other Value Disciplines*. Harvard Business Review.

CHAPTER 7

DYNAMIC CULTURE

"Culture eats strategy for lunch."—Curt Coffman

Prime the Engine: Pre-Reading Questions

1. Can you describe the culture of your organization? If so, do you like the description?

2. Do new hires remark about the organizational culture in positive terms?

3. Does the senior management team talk about culture? Does it actively manage key aspects of culture?

4. Does your culture hinder change or help drive it in adapting to new circumstances?

Your answers should be "yes" except for the last one, which you can probably guess. (That's right, help drive it.) Read on to learn about creating and maintaining a dynamic culture.

Introduction

Culture is an enterprise's operating system. It orchestrates the interactions of the enterprise's components, much as an operating system orchestrates the parts of a computer. Fast, powerful computers have fast, powerful operating systems. Energized enterprises have dynamic, vibrant, and strong cultures—lackluster, enervated enterprises don't. While organizations with weak cultures can be successful, at least in financial terms, they are generally not great places to work and perform at levels below where they could or should be.

This chapter follows the chapters on purpose, leadership, employee engagement, and customer intimacy because those both drive and are driven by an organization's culture. This chapter will show you that culture is both manageable and important to organizational success, and that weak or toxic cultures simply don't need to—and shouldn't—exist.

What Exactly Is Culture?

Louis V. Gerstner, Jr., the former CEO of IBM, once said, "The thing I have learned at IBM is that culture is everything." Gerstner had good reason to say that. IBM is perhaps the ultimate example of how culture both hinders and helps organizational success. When Gerstner joined IBM in 1993, it was a victim of its own inward-facing, product-oriented culture. The company was on a deep, downward slide that pundits said was irreversible.

Despite being mercilessly flogged by the press and analysts, Gerstner managed to turn that culture into one much more externally focused on customers and solutions, and the company not only survived but also branched into new services and markets that reinvigorated it. IBM continues to reinvent itself, most recently embracing agile practices and social collaboration. It's a remarkable transformation—especially for a company of its size.

The notion of organizational culture is relatively new, dating back to the 1980s. That means that while organizational culture has existed since humans first organized into groups to accomplish things, only recently has it been a focus of management attention. Perhaps that is why relatively few organizations have gained notoriety for their strong, dynamic cultures.

Of the many definitions of organizational culture, one that I like is: "the specific collection of values and norms that are shared by people and groups in an organization and that control the way they interact with each other and with stakeholders outside the organization," from Charles W. L. Hill, and Gareth R. Jones. An even simpler definition comes from Terrance Deal and Alan Kennedy, who describe culture as "the way things get done around here."

Culture both derives from and governs how managers and employees work, think, interact, and generally view the world. That means that culture is a key part of an organization's foundation—static, weak cultures mean weak enterprises, while strong cultures support and drive strong enterprises.

Before we go any farther, Figure 10 shows my definition of "strong" and "weak" cultures.

Figure 10: Strong and Weak Culture Comparison

Static, Weak Culture	Dynamic, Strong Culture
• Top-down leadership	• Flat, fluid leadership
• Risk-averse	• Open to experimentation
• Change-resistant	• Fluid and adaptable to change
• Employees governed by rules	• Autonomous employees
• Inwardly and product focused	• Customer-focused
• Strive to survive	• Strive for excellence

Consider an organization where the senior management team, after holding frequent meetings and off-sites, delivers new strategies as a *fait accompli*. Employees are expected to accept and execute those strategies, organization structure is rigid and siloed, and communications are laden with company-speak and jargon.

In this scenario, employees have little stake or pride in their work as it is dictated from above. They have little contact with customers, so they don't understand them very well. Changes in direction are frequent and come from the top down, and targets are missed so often that the reward/punishment management scheme resembles the "floggings will continue until morale improves" approach. That is a classic weak culture.

Now imagine a company with a strong, dynamic culture where managers and employees create strategies collaboratively. Work is accomplished by autonomous cross-functional teams, employees and managers communicate as peers using plain English, and employees come to work with a strong sense of purpose and desire to accomplish great things. Employees at all levels interact with customers, both face-to-face and via social media, and strive to provide superior products and services for them.

Chapter 2 looked at systems thinking. Cultures are systems, and fairly complex ones at that. So an organization's culture can (with enough patience) be diagrammed and modeled using the causal loops and other systems thinking artifacts described in Chapter 2. Although culture is often thought of as the "soft squishy stuff," it isn't. A skilled cultural anthropologist can readily dissect and document an organization's culture, but most employees can pretty accurately describe the cultures in which they work in at least basic terms.

Systems thinking, or a similar approach that studies the interaction of the parts that make up a system, is critical to understanding and managing organizational culture. Think about the dimensions of strong and weak cultures and how the achievement of a dynamic and strong culture requires active management of purpose, leadership, engagement, and customer focus. Great cultures don't happen by themselves—they are created and managed.

Another reason for a systems approach is that while enterprises generally have an overarching culture, their departments and units generally have their own cultures that may collide with one another. Think marketing and IT for example. Their cultures are often programmed for a collision course, as IT is process-driven and risk-averse, and most marketing organizations are not.

Being able to model and think about not only the top-level culture but also the various sub-cultures of an enterprise is important to achieving a dynamic and healthy culture.

In short, culture may be complex, but it's definable, identifiable, and understandable as a system.

Why Culture Matters

James Haskett and John Kotter, in their 1992 book, *Corporate Culture and Performance*, tracked a mix of companies over an 11-year period that either had, or didn't have, "strong cultures that facilitate adaptation to a changing world." They found that revenue growth for companies with strong cultures averaged 682%, while growth was 166% for firms without strong cultures. Net income growth during the 11-year period was 756% contrasted with 1%! Now you see the point of this chapter.

An example of the negative impact of a complacent culture is Eastman Kodak—a firm that *The Economist* called "the Google of its day." A 2012 *Economist* article described Kodak as having made significant investments in research, a rigorous approach to manufacturing, and good relations with the local community. Those are all harbingers of a successful business. What Kodak lacked was a dynamic culture that could adapt to the changing world of photography. It suffered from the double whammy of a complacent culture and executive focus on creating perfect products, and was ultimately vanquished by Fujifilm.

Hitting closer to home is a study conducted by the Yale School of Public Health that focused on patient outcomes at hospitals with strong and weak cultures. Patient death rates at the highest performing hospitals (strong culture) were half as high as at the lowest performing hospitals (weak culture). The study defined the key ingredients of strong cultures as openness, involved leadership, accountability, and interpersonal excellence. The highest performing hospitals scored high on those factors while the lesser performing hospitals did not. Leslie Curry, one of the researchers, noted, "it was not just what the hospitals were doing but how they were doing it." In other words, going back to Deal and Kennedy, "it's how things get done around here."

Culture Trumps Strategy but Together They Rock

Culture and strategy are clearly different phenomena, but they are inextricably linked. One definition of strategy, from businessdictionary.com, is "a method or plan chosen to bring about a desired future, such as achievement of a goal or solution to a problem."

Many organizations focus intense energy and resources on crafting business strategies but not on building a strong culture. My theory is that strategy is more tangible than culture and far easier to change; hence, it's more likely to be addressed. However, ignoring culture is dangerous because the existing organizational culture may not have "the right stuff" to execute the strategy. For example, a static culture will hamstring attempts to change strategy, leading to failure of an otherwise viable strategy.

The "culture eats strategy for lunch" quote at the beginning of this chapter hints that organizations with strong dynamic cultures will, over time, trump organizations that have weaker cultures but strong business strategies. I believe that's true. Strategies are ephemeral and based on current and predicted market conditions. A strong and dynamic culture can adapt to change; weak cultures generally cannot.

Witness Eastman Kodak, which made strategic shifts but didn't have the culture to drive the necessary change. Likewise, IBM, after many years of successful business strategies, fell victim to an inward-focused culture that hindered it from creating and implementing more customer-centric strategies. It only succeeded by first "fixing" its culture.

Organizations with strong business strategies will succeed until changes, either internal or external, render those strategies ineffective. Organizations with dynamic and adaptive cultures are able to respond to change and adjust strategy accordingly. Organizations with strong business strategies and cultures are the 800-pound gorillas—not only have they figured out how to compete and thrive, but they also have a cultural foundation that supports the factors necessary to implement their strategies even as they evolve.

Rather than focusing on strategy and hoping culture follows, a better approach is to build and shape culture and strategy in parallel. Culture that doesn't support business strategy is problematic, as is strategy that doesn't fit culture. Building a culture focused on achievement, flexibility, and even durability provides a foundation for the continuous change that is likely to mark the foreseeable future of business, academia, and government.

Building Blocks of Great Culture

What makes up a great organizational culture? Many opinions exist, and I'll add my own to the mix here. All organizational cultures have a fair number of moving parts. In weak cultures, those parts don't work together. In strong cultures, they dovetail and march in lockstep to support and drive the organization's business strategies. Here are seven key components of a great organizational culture:

1. **Strong sense of purpose.** Organizations with a firm *raison d'etre* tend to have stronger cultures. Refer back to the contrast between Sony and Patagonia in Chapter 3 as an example. One reason is simple—getting up in the morning to go to work for an organization whose mission is important to you is simply easier and more compelling than the alternative. The second reason is a bit more nuanced. Organizations with a strong sense of purpose become "we" organizations, because employees have a collective sense about what they are doing and why it matters.

2. **Right people in the right jobs.** I am perennially mystified that so many organizations either hire the wrong people or hire the right people and put them in the wrong jobs. I'll allow that getting the right people in the right jobs is not simple, but if an organization can't achieve that goal, success will be painful

at best and elusive at worst. There is simply no substitute for holding out for the right people and then working with them to create a mutually beneficial job situation. On the rare occasions when I hurried to hire people who didn't feel quite right, it was a mistake.

3. **Open communications.** Probably the biggest impediment to a vibrant culture is lack of clear and open communications. Symptoms include overuse of euphemisms designed to hide poor performance, over-reliance on internal jargon, and browbeating by managers that stifles conversation.

   In an organization with a strong culture, employees and managers communicate clearly, logically, and unemotionally. Discussions are fact-based and language is not laced with jargon and innuendos. Meetings are open, informal affairs that rarely involve PowerPoint presentations. In other words, people simply talk to one another clearly and succinctly.

4. **Involved leadership.** One real culture killer is "seagull managers." They are largely uninvolved in day-to-day activities, then fly in, poop all over everything, and fly out. Because of their non-involvement, seagull managers often require extensive status reporting so they can persuade their bosses that they know what's going on. Those status reports often precipitate more "flying" and, well, suffice it to say that this creates a positive feedback loop with very negative consequences.

   Contrast that with managers who, while maintaining their leadership roles, also function as team members contributing their expertise and experience to further the team's efforts. The manager doesn't need extensive status reports because he/she is involved in day-to-day activities. Not meddling, but involved as an active participant.

5. **Accountability at all levels.** If you're familiar with the Dilbert comic strip, think about Wally—the coffee-swilling engineer whose career goal seems to be avoiding work at all costs. The

insidious part of lack of accountability is that it is contagious. Who wouldn't want to avoid taking responsibility? Answer: the people you want working for you.

Organizations with strong cultures thrive on accountability—if you have built the right culture and hired the right people, they will take ownership of their work and expect others to do the same. They do so not out of fear of punishment, but because it is the right thing to do, managers provide a supportive environment, and their peers, managers, and customers are counting on them. Being accountable elevates an employee's status and doesn't mark him or her as a "sucker."

6. **Trust and interpersonal excellence.** An organization without trust could never have a healthy and dynamic culture. Francis Fukuyama, in his book *Trust*, argues that trust that goes beyond kinship was the foundation for the creation of large-scale corporations and businesses. I'd take that a step further and say that trust is the foundation of any organization's culture—it is the currency of a healthy culture. Organizations in which employees don't trust management and/or each other have a very tough row to hoe when they need to enact extreme change.

7. **External focus.** One trait I've noticed in high-performing cultures is that managers and employees are attuned to customers and what is happening in the marketplace. Yes, they mind the internal operational stuff that needs to be done well, but they spend more time looking at external conditions and making continuous adjustments to ensure that their organizations remain viable and competitive. In the best cultures, employees actually like customers and vice versa.

Note that these building blocks help create great culture and at the same time are created by great culture. In other words, they are self-reinforcing. Unfortunately, the same is true for the building blocks of weak cultures—that is why they are so hard to change.

Jazz and Zappos: Getting to the Culture You Want

Lawrence J. Peter once said, "if you don't know where you are going, you'll probably end up somewhere else." Organizational culture is a lot like that. A laissez-faire approach is like rolling the dice. You might get lucky and grow a dynamic culture, but the odds are against you. And for better or for worse, organizational cultures often reflect their leadership. If leaders are ethical, focused, humble, and dynamic, culture may reflect those values. Think Hewlett and Packard. If leaders embrace less noble values, cultures will be toxic. Think Enron and J.P. Morgan.

Culture left to "drift" will absorb the nuances of the management team and employees, both good and bad. I sometimes think of organizational culture as a battle between human frailties such as gossip, greed, jealousy, and need for power, and their nicer twins of mutual respect, sharing, giving credit, and collaboration. Culture needs to be actively monitored and managed to keep the evil twins in check.

Zappos is a company that actively manages culture—it focuses on culture as its No. 1 priority. Founder and CEO Tony Hsieh has a remarkable background, but what intrigues me most is his instinct for creating a great culture. Among the interesting examples is the Zappos "Culture Book," a compendium of employee thoughts on what they want the culture to be and where it falls short. The book signals that employees' thoughts are important, management is listening, and shortfalls are addressed. Also powerful is the notion of an "Ask Anything" newsletter where employees can ask whatever they want and get a published response. That would be anathema for many organizations.

Zappos also exhibits fanatical devotion to customer service and has gone to extraordinary lengths to ensure high levels of service. It exemplifies the belief that "your culture is your brand." Think about the companies you like and those you love to hate. Whatever you like or dislike about a given company is probably deeply embedded in its culture.

Jazz musicians are a great non-business example of dynamic culture, especially a group that doesn't usually play together in a formal band. Jazz songs are typically structured with a "head," which is a unison part played by everyone, interspersed with solos. A good jazz performance is like poetry in motion. There isn't a "leader," per se; instead, leadership is passed from a soloist back to the group, and then on to the next soloist, and so on.

While the soloist plays, the other musicians support him by playing whatever will maximize the effect of his work. That, in a nutshell, is my ideal organizational dynamic. Where culture comes into play is that the musicians share a strong and common purpose—that of providing a great experience for the audience. They also share a desire for personal and group excellence and communicate using a common language. Finally, they trust each other's abilities and are willing to sublimate individual egos to enhance the performance. That's what enables a group of talented jazz musicians to just "show up and play."

That culture is dynamic and portable; that is, the musicians can go their separate ways and re-form other groups with other musicians and achieve the same effect. Check out a jazz performance and see what you can bring back to your own organization.

For CEOs and Executives

Creating and maintaining a dynamic culture is not just a "nice-to-have" any more. A strong, dynamic culture is critical to your success, so it's time to roll up your sleeves and get to work. Where to begin? At the beginning, by gaining an objective view of your organization's culture. Not how you want it to be, but what it actually is. Here's your to-do list:

- Starting with the seven building blocks discussed in this chapter, assess your culture. Do it by yourself first, then ask your team, and finally ask employees. Note any lack of congruency between management and employee assessments. It's important for all members of the organization (especially your managers) to have a consistent view of the "baseline culture" before embarking on change initiatives.

- Look to the past. Cultures change and drift over time, If your organization used to have a strong culture but now doesn't, identify what changed in the environment that led to that weakening.

- Look to the future. Create your own building blocks. What do you want and need your culture to be? Map your business strategy to your culture—does the culture support and drive the strategy, and vice versa?

- Find an anchor. Even weak cultures usually have some good points. Seize onto those and use them as a toehold to drive change in other areas.

- Be patient and celebrate small victories. Changing culture takes time, and trying to fix everything at once will lead to endless frustration. Start with small, finite changes and keep chipping away.

- Finally, show your passion. It's pretty hard for employees to be passionate about their organizations and their work if management doesn't display that passion.

As noted earlier, while many regard culture as difficult to pin down, a rigorous approach to understanding and management can work wonders. Just ask Lou Gerstner of IBM. Above all, for executives, culture is either a millstone that thwarts change and adaptation, or it is the wellspring of success—it's that important.

For Team Leaders and Business Unit Managers

If you are a leader or manager of a business unit or team that has a toxic culture within a larger organization that has a healthy culture, I have bad news. The problem is likely you and your managers, if you have any. If the reverse is true, I have good news—it is possible to create and manage a healthy culture even in a larger dysfunctional or toxic organization. Not easy, but possible. Here's what you need to do:

- Look at the big picture. Understand the dynamics of the larger organization—good, bad, and indifferent. In other words, know what you are up against. Also, find at least one redeeming quality of the larger culture and embed it into your culture. Linkage is important.

- Hire the right people—no shortcuts and no compromises. One bad apple spoils the barrel, and one toxic employee can poison a surprisingly large number of workers.

- Work with staff to ensure fitness in their roles. Going back to Chapter 5's notions of autonomy, mastery, and purpose, "audit" your various roles to see how they fit. When they don't, work with the incumbents to achieve that fit.

- Like executives, front-line managers need to have and show passion. If yours is lacking, find ways to recharge and re-invigorate it before embarking on any cultural change initiatives.

Living Dynamic Culture

Even if companies with healthy cultures didn't outperform those with weaker cultures, I'd vote hands down to work for the outfits with healthy cultures. So will most smart, ambitious workers—the people you want to hire. As we've seen, healthy cultures do outperform weak ones, so I'm at a loss to understand why organizations don't work to create those healthy environments. Companies like Zappos, Apple, and Southwest Airlines celebrate healthy, dynamic cultures—and that celebration is part of the culture itself, feeding a continuous cycle of renewal and re-energizing.

As we saw in the jazz musician example, collaboration is a key part of a dynamic culture, so in Chapter 8 I'll dig deeper into collaboration.

Resources

- Curry, L. A., E. Spatz, E. Cherlin, et. al. "What Distinguishes Top-Performing Hospitals in Acute Myocardial Infarction Mortality Rates?" *Annals of Internal Medicine*, March 15, 2011.

- Deal, T. E., and A.A. Kennedy. 1982. *Corporate Cultures: The Rites and Rituals of Corporate Life.* Harmondsworth: Penguin Books. Reissue 2000, Perseus Books.

- Hill, Charles W. L., and Gareth R. Jones. 2001. *Strategic Management.* Houghton Mifflin.

- Hsieh, Tony. 2010. *Delivering Happiness: A Path to Profits, Passion, and Purpose.* Business Plus.

- Kotter, John, and Heskett, James L. 1992. *Corporate Culture and Performance.* Free Press.

- Parr, Shawn. "Culture Eats Strategy for Lunch." *Fast Company*, January 24, 2012.

- "The Last Kodak Moment." *The Economist*, January 14, 2012.

CHAPTER 8

ENTERPRISE COLLABORATION

"Alone we can do so little, together we can do so much."—Helen Keller

Prime the Engine: Pre-Reading Questions

1. Do your reward structures favor individual or team contributions, or both?

2. Is collaboration among employees ad hoc or based on established practices and tools?

3. Is the senior management team collaborative? Do they work together, across functions, to achieve organizational goals?

4. Do employees and managers collaborate with customers and partners on new product initiatives?

Correct answers are 1) both, 2) established practices and tools, 3) yes, and 4) yes. If that doesn't describe your organization, read on.

Introduction

So far we've looked at establishing smart work practices, compelling purpose, focused leadership, engaged employees, customer intimacy, and dynamic culture. The next logical step is creating a collaborative enterprise.

Collaboration is nothing new, but enterprise collaboration is nascent; in fact, consider this chapter an introduction to a phenomenon that is still unfolding. I'm bullish on enterprise collaboration because a perfect storm of forces is driving organizations to move from siloed, hierarchical structures to flatter, networked or "mesh" organizations. That perfect storm consists of cloud computing, mobile devices, Web 2.0, and changes in the dynamics of workplaces and society, as we'll see later in this chapter.

These collaborative enterprises will be flat (as opposed to hierarchical), with fluid dynamics and structure and self-forming teams and organizations that coalesce around problems and opportunities. As an example, think of an organization where employees work together to solve problems and exploit opportunities, much like white blood cells pile on invading diseases until they are eradicated, then move on to the next. The worker white blood cells don't wait for a management cell to tell them to attack—they know what to do. If you have successfully implemented the suggestions in the earlier chapters, then your employees are like those white blood cells—they know what to do.

This chapter contains a quick overview and history of collaboration, some thoughts about where it is going, and my advice on how to move toward a collaborative enterprise. To start, let's take a brief look at the definition and history of collaboration in the workplace.

Defining Enterprise Collaboration

Of the many definitions of enterprise collaboration, I like Oracle's: "a process in which the *right* people connect with the *right* expertise or information at the *right* time to drive the *right* business decision." That's a good meat and potatoes definition, but it also feels a bit sterile. I think of collaborative enterprises as places where the culture, purpose, leadership, tools, and people come together to make it possible for teams of any size to accomplish more than they could by working individually.

Think back to the 1+1=3 organizations I talked about in Chapter 1—enterprise collaboration is key to those energized enterprises.

Why Collaborative Enterprises are Emerging and What They Look Like

Collaboration in the workplace is a topic that has kicked into overdrive in recent years. Why? Chalk it up to four primary forces that have collided: cloud computing, mobile computing, Web 2.0 and Enterprise 2.0, and substantive shifts in social and workplace behaviors.

Figure 11: Forces Behind Enterprise Collaboration

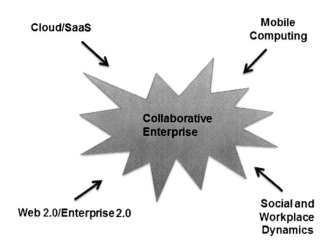

Cloud computing is the delivery of computing services over the Internet. It enables fast and often inexpensive deployment of applications including social and collaborative tools. That means that IT organizations have less work to do to implement collaborative applications, and in some cases aren't involved at all (although non-involvement is not necessarily recommended).

Web and Enterprise 2.0 are based on a collection of technologies including blogs, wikis, microblogs, social sharing and tagging, and syndication, to name a few. Web 2.0 is the external manifestation, characterized by Twitter, Facebook, and LinkedIn. Enterprise 2.0 refers to the same types of technologies used within enterprises to foster collaboration and communication.

Mobile devices help foster collaboration as many workers today are working remotely and/or traveling. The emergence of smart, powerful devices has empowered the notion of "going Bedouin," or working in a nomadic style that is not based on the use of an office. A key component of enterprise collaboration is anywhere/anytime access.

Social and workplace dynamics, simply put, have changed and are driving much change in organizations. Younger, more tech-savvy and socially oriented employees are insisting on bringing the ways in which they collaborate in their personal lives into the workplace. They also expect to use Facebook, LinkedIn, and Twitter, or at least tools that look and function similarly. These tools don't supplant phones and face-to-face meetings, at least for now, and they shouldn't. There is, and I believe always will be, value in live communication, as you'll see later in my example of a collaborative project.

The confluence of forces that are driving collaboration are breaking down silos and hierarchical command and control enterprises where only certain departments interact with customers. Figure 12 illustrates the difference in structure and communications in traditional and collaborative enterprises.

Figure 12: Hierarchical vs. Collaborative Communication

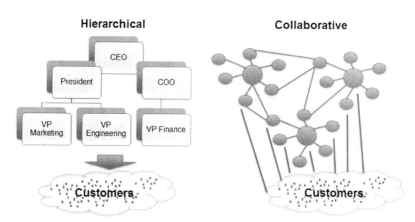

If your organization looks like the one on the left, you are comfortably in the mainstream and you might think that is cause not to undertake creation of a collaborative enterprise. However, if your competition, existing or yet unseen, looks like the organization on the right, I would submit you will soon be "living in interesting times" (and not in a good way). That is because collaborative organizations—your competition—can:

- Make decisions more quickly by moving decision-making out to the "edge" where customers live

- Harvest new ideas from customers, partners, and even competitors instead of relying on employees and managers for innovation

- Locate information and expertise quickly and easily, ensuring that decisions are made by the best-equipped people with the best information available

- Create energy levels that are not achievable by siloed and singular working approaches

In short, collaborative enterprises have several advantages over their traditional counterparts. The time dimension is also important.

Creating a collaborative enterprise from scratch can be done quickly, while moving an existing organization from the left to the right of the diagram takes time—in some cases, a lot of time.

Why You Need to Get Collaborative

Let's get down to brass tacks—why enterprise collaboration matters to you and your organization. Simply, organizations that don't make the shift will be unable to compete in increasingly chaotic and fast-moving markets. Enterprise collaboration is essential because we aren't solving the same problems now that we were in the previous century, as the lists in Figure 13 show:

Figure 13: Shifting Business Challenges

Last century	This century
• Quality control	• Communicating and maintaining vision and goals
• Supply chain optimization	• Finding and retaining specialized talent
• Cost minimization	• Finding and sharing information and expertise
• Manufacturing efficiencies	• Anticipating and reacting to change, being agile
• Globalization	• Retaining and engaging customers and partners
• Customer attraction	• Improving speed of communication and decision making
• Brand development	• Brand management

Note that in Figure 13 the list on the left is heavy on process optimization, cost control, and traditional marketing. That isn't to say that collaboration doesn't work or help in such environments—re-read the Chapter 2 discussion on lean thinking and you'll see that collaboration is essential.

Moving to the right column, the items are much more focused on people, expertise, and information, as those are the actual products and services many firms provide. Instead of maximizing efficiency in production, the problem *du jour* is finding and maximizing the effective use of talent, a much different problem and one that requires—not just benefits from—collaborative technologies and cultures to solve.

If we aren't solving the same needs and problems, then clearly the same tools, work practices, and management techniques are not going to work. Borrowing from the movie *Jaws*, we may not need a bigger boat, but we do need a different one.

A Quick Personal History of Enterprise Collaboration

When I joined the workforce back in the 1970s, I worked in an office using a calculator to get through page after page of calculations on airline fuel consumption. "Social computing" consisted of talking to other employees while standing in line to use the punch card reader.

Collaboration was done via live meetings and phone calls, and tended to be somewhat formal. Challenging one's boss in a meeting was a bit like taunting a bear—you might survive, but it was an experience you wouldn't forget.

Fast forward to the mid-1980s, and I was responsible for implementing IBM's e-mail and calendaring solution, along with its solution for sharing documents, at a major utility. Both ran on incredibly expensive mainframes and had character-based, not graphical, interfaces, but they did foster the ability to schedule meetings, share information across geographies, and conduct online dialogues. This was the dawn of computer-enabled collaboration.

In the mid-to-late 1990s, I used video and audio conferencing, chat, and instant messaging to coordinate activities in real-time for geographically dispersed teams. That enabled live discussions across time zones and geographies and also fostered new project management practices such as agile development, discussed in Chapter 2. My earliest real collaboration successes were in agile web development projects. But I still feel there's a lot more to collaboration that is yet untapped.

We are still in the early phases of enterprise collaboration. While there has been an explosion of tools to support collaboration of all types, the uptake and adoption has been somewhat slower. Figure 14 shows examples of collaboration tools.

Figure 14: Collaboration Tools

- Blogs
- Wikis
- Micro-blogs
- Discussion forums
- Syndication
- News feed aggregation
- Personal dashboards
- Instant messaging
- Social networks
- Media sharing
- Social review and rating
- Bookmarking, tagging
- Idea banks
- Prediction markets

Clearly, a wide variety of solutions exists for all types of collaboration. So why did market research firm Forrester find that only 28% of knowledge workers use social (collaboration) software at least monthly? Because, in addition to tools, enterprise collaboration requires a culture that supports, enables, and drives it. Figure 15 lists some of the principles that define a collaboration-friendly culture.

Figure 15: Principles of Collaboration

- Transparency
- Engagement
- Cooperation
- Sharing
- Transformation
- Wisdom of crowds
- Democratic
- Participative
- Trust
- Co-innovation

Note that earlier chapters of this book discuss many of these principles: they are foundational to the creation of an energized enterprise and to enterprise collaboration. That means you need to take a hard look at your organization and identify areas needing remediation before you jump into enterprise collaboration.

That said, collaboration can be a tool to help build strength in these areas—they don't all have to be "perfect" before you jump in. What's important is to know where you are weak and focus on using collaboration to bolster those weaknesses.

Examples of Successful Collaboration

As I noted earlier, some of my most successful collaborative experiences have involved teams that coalesced around creating or rebuilding websites. A particularly good one involved creating, from scratch, a corporate website that also fulfilled products, in this case, digital reports, blog posts, and data. Two particular challenges for this initiative were integrating staff from two outside vendors, and the team's distribution across four locations.

The approach was agile, as described in Chapter 2, and the team included marketing, web production, developers, and user interface specialists and graphic designers. The wrinkle was that the site had to be completed in less than 90 days for showing at a conference.

The collaborative aspects were several.

First, the team was cross-functional but we adopted fairly loose role definitions, focusing on who was best suited to perform a given task.

Lesson learned—people know a lot more than their positions or titles would indicate. We gained a lot of creativity from not enforcing roles. Let people rise to the occasion and do what they do best.

Second, we used a series of tools from 37signals including Campfire, a chat room with document-sharing, to create a virtual bullpen environment. While the tools supported day-to-day communication and collaboration, our most important decision was to gather the team in one location at the outset to build relationships before relying on the collaboration tools.

Lesson learned—collaboration works a lot better if people have some face time to get to know each other.

Third, in classical agile fashion, we used bi-weekly iterations, daily stand-up meetings, and iteration kickoffs and reviews to structure the project. We were able to quickly move from concept to design to development, and the resulting website launch was anticlimactic, as stakeholders had watched it being built.

Lesson learned—collaboration needs structure and rhythm. Free-form collaboration generates a lot of activity but will likely not accomplish as much as an orchestrated approach.

My example is relatively small-scale, and in fact that is a good place to start, but there are a number of successful enterprise examples on a much larger scale. One is IBM's move to what it calls a social business and I call a collaborative enterprise.

How IBM Did It

By using IBM as an example, I'm not implying that only big, tech-savvy companies can become collaborative enterprises. IBM largely followed the same path that much smaller organizations would follow, just on a dramatically larger scale.

First, IBM's leadership embraced the need for social collaboration and recognized that it required a long and sustained effort to get there.

Second, it emphasized the need to integrate social collaboration into existing processes and tools, using a three-pronged approach:

- Leadership drives the collaboration initiatives

- HR supports the necessary cultural changes

- IT provides the necessary tools

Third, and possibly most important, IBM emphasized the need for the three parties to coordinate. For example, HR needs to work with leadership to ensure that the expansion of social cultures is tied to practical and significant business priorities. And both parties need to work closely with IT to ensure the adoption of appropriate tools.

It is interesting to note that IBM's move to social collaboration works within the framework of leadership, HR, and IT; in other words, the traditional organizational structure. IBM also used some fairly simple and pragmatic approaches, including having leadership spearhead a move from e-mail to collaborative tools and having HR provide incentives to employees who leverage collaboration. Finally, tying back to Chapter 7's customer intimacy theme, much of IBM's focus has been on collaboration with customers and partners, not just employees and managers.

Building Blocks of Enterprise Collaboration

Effective enterprise collaboration requires an orchestrated approach. While some level of collaboration happens naturally in most organizations, putting structure and management into place will yield better results. Here are some key building blocks:

Have a plan. Gartner has estimated that 70% of all social initiatives (including enterprise collaboration) fail. That's enough to stop many in their tracks, but failure isn't a foregone conclusion. The old adage that "failure to plan is planning to fail" applies in spades here. Successful collaboration initiatives are undergirded by clearly defined business problems and objectives, and plans and road maps for execution.

What gets measured gets managed. Another key ingredient for enterprise collaboration is metrics than can be used to manage and gauge the success of initiatives. How can you know if you succeeded if you haven't defined success in some measurable way?

You trust me, I trust you. Trust is a key element of successful collaboration. If collaborators feel that they are being tracked and monitored by management, failure is imminent. Management trust is imperative, as some managers view social and collaborative tools as games or time wasters, and that is the ultimate buzz kill. To be sure, some employees will make these tools time wasters, but if that's your concern let me direct you back to Chapter 5 on employee engagement.

The chicken is involved, the pig is committed. The old joke about a bacon-and-egg breakfast makes an important point about the difference between involvement and commitment. Management needs to be *committed* to collaboration. Committed means participating, not watching. If your company introduces a collaboration tool like Yammer or Google+, make sure you lead the way in using it. Managers need to be thought leaders in using collaboration to solve business challenges and communicate with customers.

I can speak clearly now. Clear, unconstrained communications are a cornerstone of collaboration. Communications laden with corporate jargon and management-speak and constrained by policies and procedures will diffuse energy and degrade performance. A 2010 Harris Interactive survey found that only 8% of companies were seen as effective in internal communications and only 7% of employees felt that co-workers understood their skill sets. Note that communication is a two-way street, and I suspect that as much as clear communication is problematic, so is listening, or lack thereof.

The right tool for the right job. One key reason that collaboration initiatives fail is that the tools are not appropriate for the task at hand and/or they are not integrated into workflows. Employees don't want another application; they want to be able to collaborate within the tools and environments they already use. They also don't want to learn new interfaces—they already know how to use Facebook, Twitter, and Wikipedia. To the extent that you can mimic the look and feel of familiar social applications *and* embed them into existing online work tools, collaboration will be more successful.

For CEOs and Executives

Transforming an organization from one that collaborates only casually and in ad hoc applications to one in which collaboration is a culture and discipline will not happen overnight. Nor will it necessarily "stick" once it's done. Research shows that organizations that have achieved higher levels of collaboration can backslide if not managed. The implication is that attaining enterprise collaboration requires sustained management and attention, and unless you are willing to commit to that, the results will be less than successful. Your to-do list:

- Understand why you are pursuing enterprise collaboration, and define goals and the desired end state. Collaboration means many things to many people, and lack of shared understanding will lead to a shotgun approach.

- Get objective assistance in looking at your organization in terms of its ability to support large-scale collaboration. Don't use tools to try to drive collaboration in an environment that isn't ready—it won't work.

- Start small and don't overdo it. Learn from IBM and pick themes such as moving away from e-mail to collaboration tools, or creating social networks with customers.

- Don't just support collaboration, be part of it. Better yet, be a leader in the use of collaborative tools and practices.

- Weave collaboration tools into the fabric of corporate communications and turn top-down information blasts into conversations with employees.

- Create environments where customers, managers, and employees can share ideas. Make the results of those collaborations highly visible.

- Make collaboration and sharing part of your hiring profile and have HR create rewards for collaborative behaviors.

For Team Leaders and Business Unit Managers

I've had the challenging role of creating and managing collaborative organizations in companies that are distinctly non-collaborative. Doing so means compromising some of the core tenets of collaboration, and also picking and choosing those outside your team with whom you collaborate in the fullest sense. But that shouldn't stop you from pursuing better collaboration—it's too important. Your to-do list:

- Start with a basic business problem or opportunity, create a business case, select tools, and finally create a road map for execution. Be prepared to make course corrections—it's part of the process.

- Find teams or groups that are predisposed to using social software to participate in pilots or initial implementation phases.

- Partner with your IT organization. You will need their help, even if you plan to use cloud-based collaboration applications, as integrating those with existing applications is key to driving usage.

- Provide some basic "rules of the road" for use of collaborative tools and practices—don't make your staff figure it out on their own. This applies both to internal collaboration tools and (especially) customer-facing ones.

- As in the advice to executives, take a leadership role in using collaborative tools and practices. Collaboration is not a spectator sport.

- Call attention to successes and recognize those who really get leverage out of collaboration.

Living Enterprise Collaboration

Walk into an organization that truly embraces enterprise collaboration and you'll see an entirely different animal than one that doesn't. Energy levels are high because of a strong sense of shared purpose, awareness of how each person's work contributes to the greater good, sensitivity to customer needs, and dramatically less focus on inward-facing activities. It's a safe bet that people who work for these organizations will never return to those that don't embrace collaboration.

If you choose not to become a collaborative enterprise, you will be trying to find new hires in a talent pool that is not only shrinking, but also increasingly comprised of less attractive candidates.

Next, I'll look at technology as an engine for energized enterprises, including some technologies mentioned in this chapter.

Resources

- Buhin, Jacques, and Michael Chui. September 2009. *How Companies are Benefitting from Web 2.0*. McKinsey Global Survey, McKinsey Quarterly.

- Chiu, Michael, and James Manyika. July 2012. *The Social Economy: Unlocking Value and Productivity Through Social Technologies*. McKinsey Global Institute.

- Datta, Lokesh. December 25, 2010. *Darwin to Dilbert: Contextualizing Top Collaboration Quotes*. All Collaboration.

- Datta, Lokesh, and Steve Lamont. 2010. *Assessing the State of Collaboration: Return to Essentials*. All Collaboration.

- IBM Corp. 2011. *Jamming on Social Business: Exploring New Approaches for the Next Era of Business*.

- IBM Corp. 2011. *The Social Business: Advent of a New Age*.

CHAPTER 9

TRANSFORMATIONAL TECHNOLOGY

"Any technology distinguishable from magic is insufficiently advanced."—Barry Gehm

Prime the Engine: Pre-Reading Questions

1. In your organization, does technology drive business decisions or does business drive technology decisions?

2. Does your technology infrastructure often hinder your ability to implement new products and services?

3. Is technology a "sore topic" at management meetings?

4. Does your use of technology put you ahead of competitors, and is it in line with market expectations?

Your answers should be 1) both, 2) no, 3) no, and 4) yes. If not, read this chapter and transform!

Introduction

I like Barry Gehm's quote, a corollary of Arthur C. Clarke's original, because it reflects much of what I observe about the way enterprises use technology.

When I speak about the power of technology to energize organizations, many listeners look at me like I have two heads. That's because they are thinking about IT at their organizations: cryptic and tedious user application interfaces, multiple IDs and passwords to remember, unresponsive IT support staff, and boat anchor laptops—the things they deal with each workday.

Yes, those are far from energizing—in fact, they suck energy *out* of technology users. But it doesn't have to be that way. Technologies can energize enterprises—just hand an iPad to a child to get a glimpse of what I mean.

I made technology the last "engine" in this book not because it lacks importance but rather because successful technology use is predicated on having compelling purpose, focus, engaged employees, and the other engines in place. Many organizations succumb to "shiny object syndrome" and buy technology products that promise to fix whatever ails them. Buying technology may be easier than dealing with people and with organizational shortcomings, but in my experience, it doesn't solve those problems on its own.

In this chapter, I show how your organization can get to the point where technology is working for you and not the other way around.

Defining the Problem

For many organizations, technology is the bane, not boon, of their existence. Despite the wide and growing availability of powerful technology solutions, relatively few organizations have figured out how to leverage technology for maximum advantage. Most of them use technology in a fragmented fashion to enable their business strategies. They identify a business problem, search for a technology solution, and add it into the mix of solutions they've already assembled.

The result is an enervating, frustrating patchwork of tools. I know, because I inherited a number of these throughout my career. They can be mind-numbingly complex, and are always a drag on the business.

Fortunately, there's a better way to take advantage of technology. For energized enterprises, technology isn't just an enabler of business strategy—it's the catalyst for new products, services, ways of doing business, and revenue. Combined with the other seven engines of energized enterprises, technology can provide explosive energy that transforms enterprises and drives superior performance.

Most enterprises struggle to master even the basics of aligning technology and business strategies for business impact, let alone harvest the true potential. Meta Group states that only 15% of organizations produce aligned business and IT strategies, 75% have an IT strategy but it's not aligned to business plans, and 10% have no IT strategic plan at all.

Yet, the Harvard Business Review reported that organizations that manage their IT assets well get returns as much as 40% higher than their competitors that don't. Think about that for a moment. If your organization is in the latter category, what would attaining that 40% lift look like? And according to Meta Group, organizations that have integrated IT/business strategies are 87% more likely to produce more profit than their peers, while those that don't are 82% more likely to produce less profit.

For years, the Holy Grail for CIOs has been alignment of business and IT strategy. The case for alignment is strong, but only the starting point. What you're really looking for is synergy. But I'm getting ahead of myself.

Identifying Business and Technology Strategy Disconnects

The first step in rectifying technology and business strategy disconnects is to recognize that you have a problem. Technology deficiencies can be massively visible or they can be of the "death by a thousand cuts" variety. The latter is more insidious and dangerous as it slowly saps energy and performance over time, often unnoticed.

Some common symptoms of poor strategy alignment include the following:

- Business initiatives are stymied because existing technology solutions can't support them.

- Employees complain about systems and/or lack of support hampering their work.

- Technology investments and ongoing costs seem high relative to their benefits.

- Systems and services are delivered too slowly to meet the business's needs.

- Technology initiatives don't tie well to broader corporate goals and priorities.

- Relationships between business units and technology organizations are strained or limited.

- The IT organization is unable to deliver timely information needed to run the business.

- Projects and products are mistargeted, late, or over budget, and innovation in products and services is weak or missing.

What's the best way to identify business/technology strategy issues? One way is to do it yourself. Another is to hire a consultant like me to conduct an independent assessment. I use an interview-based approach to assess how well technology is positioned to support an organization's mission and goals.

Regardless of how you approach the assessment, it is important to look at technology, and the technology organization, in the context of the business. In other words, think of the first seven engines as the context within which technology must work.

A Better Way to Develop Business and Technology Strategy

The way most enterprises approach strategy development is what causes the disconnects between business and technology. Technology today is not just a foundational element to a company's operations. It is (or should be) a key element in the company's business strategies and operations. Almost all aspects of an organization fundamentally depend on technology.

Yet, in many enterprises, technology strategies result from business strategies rather than driving them. Technology strategy is often shaped by corporate technologists based on their interpretation of what business managers are asking for. That approach may have worked 20 years ago (although from my experience, it didn't work all that well even then) but it is a death knell for modern enterprises.

Why? By the time business units formulate their strategies, then articulate them to the IT or product development folks, who then develop their plans (likely based on misinterpretations of the business strategies) which ultimately become projects, the whole world has changed. That means technology dollars are wasted solving the wrong problems and chasing the wrong opportunities.

That sort of bucket-brigade approach to planning is too slow and rife with potential for misinterpretation. More importantly, it also means technology misses the opportunity to play a transformational role in business strategy. And remember, in the most competitive, high-performing enterprises, technology doesn't just support the business—it drives the business.

From Alignment to Push-Pull Strategy Development

Organizations that fail to use technology to innovate will underperform their competition. Businesses need to move beyond simply aligning technology and business strategies, to synchronize and couple them in a way that yields synergies.

Figure 16 shows the progression from alignment to transformational strategy development. First, it shows the linear "technology follows business" approach. As noted earlier, Meta Group says 15% of organizations have attained alignment.

The highest-performing organizations, a rarefied group, have achieved the highest level of maturity—synergy—where technology and business strategy are intertwined, drive each other, and are built out in an iterative fashion.

Figure 16: Stages of Business and Technology Strategy: Functional View

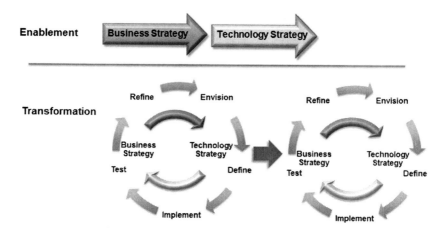

The differences between the stages are not just procedural or structural; the very focus and level of impact of each approach differs significantly, as shown in Figure 17.

Figure 17: Business and Technology Strategy: Stages of Maturity

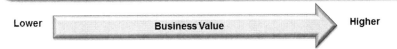

Enablement
- Business strategy drives technology strategy
- Strategy development is sequential
- IT is order taker and service provider
- Focus on delivering applications, running infrastructure, and services
- Business strategy enablement

Transformation
- Business and technology strategy push-pull each other
- Strategy development is iterative
- IT is a center of innovation
- Focus on outcomes
- Business strategy transformation

Lower ⟶ **Business Value** ⟶ Higher

As organizations move from left to right the value and impact of technology grows, evolving from business enablement to business transformation. At the enablement stage, the technology organization is an order taker, providing applications and services that answer articulated business needs but not adding technology-driven innovation.

At the transformation stage, business and technology strategies evolve iteratively in a continuous push-pull process where they build upon one another. Enablement is necessary for solving business problems; transformation is essential for leading the pack in product innovation and customer experience.

Here are a couple of examples. Procter & Gamble has introduced Business Sphere, a collection of technologies that provides executives and managers with a near-real-time view of the 4 billion times a day consumers use P&G products. The application combines massive data aggregation with visualization and analytics to facilitate decision-making in minutes, not the weeks and months it previously took. Business Sphere enables P&G to run its core business more effectively.

Kicking things up a notch, UK telecom company giffgaff is using Lithium's social media technology to create "the telecom company run by you." Its customers are also its customer service function, with 100% of customer questions answered by the community. Lithium provides the underlying technology and community management services. Customer satisfaction is an astounding 92%—that for a telecom company! Without Lithium's technology, giffgaff could not exist in its current form. Technology transforms giffgaff from a traditional telecom company to a socially driven one.

It is important to understand when a technology is being used as an enabler versus a transformation agent, as the approaches and desired results can be quite different. P&G's initiative, while substantial, did not require significant changes to organization or operations. Giffgaff's approach, on the other hand, has significant impact on people, organization structure, and business practices, since it effectively lets the company do without a traditional customer service department.

With the organization's business and technology strategy ducks in a row, it's time to look at a few energizing technologies.

Three Transformational Technologies

Many technologies have the potential to transform an organization. For the sake of brevity, I'll spotlight three that have impact and staying power, and can drive energy levels in enterprises:

- Cloud computing

- Enterprise collaboration and social CRM

- Mobile and location-based computing

Cloud Computing

In a few short years, cloud computing has gone from hype to reality, with spending on it expected to top $109 billion this year and $200 billion by 2016, according to Gartner Group. While cloud computing has been variously defined, my definition is simply "computing services provided via the Internet, generally sold on a subscription basis." One of the challenges of understanding cloud computing is that there are quite a few variations—here I focus on three that I consider important:

Software as a Service: (SaaS): the application is accessed via a website (think of Gmail, for example) and doesn't need to be loaded on everyone's computers, resulting in lower up-front costs, less implementation time and effort, and reduced maintenance.

Infrastructure as a Service (IaaS): this provides online computing power so you only pay for the capacity you need, reducing costs while providing the ability to dynamically grow or shrink computing power to meet needs.

Platform as a Service (PaaS): this provides cloud-based (rather than individual-computer-based) development environments to facilitate rapid development, testing, and deployment of applications using cutting-edge tools.

Beyond the benefits noted, cloud computing is an energizing technology because it lets enterprises rethink what they do and how they do it. In other words, it has transformational properties. Based on that view, here are different ways to look at how technology supports and drives the business:

- Technology decision-making can be moved from IT closer to business units, where it is more likely to drive change.

- IT can shift more budget from running the railroad to R&D, focusing on new product and service innovation.

- IT can shift from enforcer and gatekeeper to enabler and transformation agent.

- Online communities and self-service can reduce support costs while improving quality.

Note that many of these prompt changes in relationships between IT and business units, as IT moves from keeping the lights on and enforcing standards to helping solve business challenges and identify new revenue opportunities. This represents a potential shift for IT from operational work to product and service innovation. Note, too, IT's use of communities to offload service and support while improving service levels. All of these have significant potential to drive transformation and inject energy into enterprises.

Enterprise 2.0 and Social CRM

In Chapter 8, I discussed enterprise collaboration as an engine; here I describe some tools that support collaboration. Enterprise 2.0—or enterprise collaboration—and Social CRM are two sides of the same coin. Both employ technologies from Web 2.0 such as blogs, microblogs, wikis, tagging and sharing, and streams or feeds, but Enterprise 2.0 focuses on communication and collaboration among employees (internal) while Social CRM focuses on communication and collaboration with customers and prospects (external).

Enterprise collaboration initiatives use tools such as Jive, Yammer, and Chatter that bring Facebook and Twitter-like functionality to applications such as expertise location, document and project collaboration, and crowdsourcing. These exemplify the tools and applications that underlie enterprise collaboration as described in Chapter 8.

Social CRM initiatives, on the other hand, leverage traditional customer relationship management (CRM) tools along with social listening platforms such as Lithium, Radian6, and Jive for applications like brand management, customer sentiment tracking, and customer support communities. The tools enable harvesting and analysis of large amounts of social media to make sense of what's happening outside of the four walls of the enterprise. These tools and applications are part of the foundation for customer intimacy described in Chapter 7.

While some executives are skeptical of social technologies, they might want to look at statistics from a McKinsey survey (69% of respondents report that their companies have gained measurable business benefits from using social technologies) or MIT (employees with the most extensive digital networks were 7% more productive than their colleagues) before making up their minds. The McKinsey Global Institute further estimated that adoption of social technologies could improve productivity by 25% among knowledge workers (employees who work with information).

Mobile and Location-Based Computing

Many of the world's occupants will never own a PC; their first access to the Internet will be via a smartphone. eMarketer estimates that over 4.3 billion people use mobile phones. That means they won't have the expectations and filters built up by using PCs—they will expect all Internet interactions and transactions to be geared for mobile devices such as smartphones and tablets.

Mobile technology has three main areas of value to those trying to energize their organizations: 1) serving as a vehicle for communication and collaboration among employees, 2) serving as a vehicle for collaboration with customers, and 3) providing a platform to transform products and services. The first two are arguably enabling applications, while the latter is transformational. Since I have already discussed collaborative applications, I'll focus on products and services.

Mobile devices offer several opportunities for transformation of products and services. First, they're mobile, so they are almost always with your customers. Second, with built-in GPS capabilities, they support localized marketing and service provision. Finally, they are a platform for running apps that sell, deliver, service, and upsell your products and services.

In 2010, eBay customers bought over $2 billion in goods and services using mobile phones. In three short years, Foursquare has scaled to 250,000 merchants and over 2.5 million check-ins per day. By adding an "explore" function that allows users to search for businesses in close proximity, founder Dennis Crowley says, "you are walking down the street where you normally eat lunch. Foursquare will tell you that you're close to a sandwich place you read about in the New York Times."

The upshot is that businesses have an almost-always-on platform for delivering information, marketing content, and online products and services to individuals *in the context of their location and possibly even their current activity*. Enterprises previously tied to online sites accessed by PCs and/or brick and mortar stores have a whole new treasure trove of ways to create cross-channel customer experiences. Foursquare and eBay are the tip of the iceberg for exciting uses of mobile technology.

Building Blocks of Transformational Technology

The ability to use technology strategy as a transformational element is crucial for any enterprise and will increasingly be necessary not just to thrive, but to survive. In this section, I list key building blocks of transformational technology that organizations of all sizes and stripes can and should adopt:

- **Push-Pull Iterative Strategy Development:** Developing transformational technology and business strategies requires a fresh approach that sometimes has business driving technology selection and sometimes has technology driving business strategy decisions.

- **Periodic "blow up the business/blue sky" working sessions:** Management teams tend toward inbred thinking over time, and business strategy becomes a fine-tuning exercise rather than a true strategic assessment and overhaul of the business. Periodic "if we were starting a business today, what would it look like" sessions are a good way to spark new thinking.

- **Governance:** Governance is a fancy word for making sure that IT investments and resources are focused on projects that have business value and are prioritized so that the highest-value projects are done first. Best-practice governance uses cross-functional teams of executives.

- **Rolling budgets:** Annual budgets are a surprisingly strong inhibitor to iterative, synergistic strategy development. An alternative is to use rolling budgets, which are reviewed and adjusted quarterly to ensure that budgets (or lack thereof) are not stifling critical innovation.

- **Quarterly planning sessions:** Many companies still use annual plans, which, while better than the 5-year plans of a few years ago, are still not agile enough for today's dynamic business environments. Quarterly reviews and updates, including an honest appraisal of how current objectives, directions, and initiatives are working, can help enterprises deal with change and uncertainty in the marketplace.

- **Living enterprise architecture:** Enterprise architectures define the arrangement and interactions of computing systems needed to run the business. While they are often conceived as static documents, a better approach is a continuous review and update process to incorporate business strategy changes and developments in technology.

- **Emerging and disruptive technology sessions:** Technology is everyone's job—executives can no longer leave decisions up to technology staff. To increase business managers' technology acumen, IT or outside experts can provide "schooling" on new and complex technologies.

- **Move from project to theme focus:** While it may seem like wordplay, moving from a strict project focus to a broader "theme" focus can help both business and technology staff to think in more strategic terms. For example, contrast the project "implement a CRM system" with the theme "improve customer experience." Granted, a CRM system is a key part of managing customer experience, but focusing on that broader theme encourages staff to think about the wider implications of what they are working on.

Above all, it's key for business and technology executives and staff to embrace the need to work together, fluidly and organically, to shape and refine their business vision and strategies.

For CEOs and Executives

Technology is a powerful and essential tool for transforming an organization. But achieving that transformation requires learning and discipline. Your to-do list:

- Build a strong working relationship with your technology leader and insist that your team do the same. If the technology leader is not able to meet halfway and provide strategic and innovative direction, find a replacement fast—it's that important.

- Invest in making sure your technologists understand your business and customers as well as the markets you operate in.

- Leverage the knowledge of your technology leader—he or she gets to look at the ugly underside of your organization every day and likely knows more about how the company works than you do.

- Make technology your friend, not your nemesis. Invest your own time in becoming more tech-savvy and build technology into your business strategy planning.

- View technology as a revenue generator, not a cost center. The latter focus results in a death spiral where cost-cutting reduces IT effectiveness, causing more cost-cutting.

For Team Leaders and Business Unit Managers

Transformational technologies don't have to entail large investments, especially in this era of open-source technology. Getting results does require vision and discipline, though. Your to-do list:

- Like senior management, invest time in building a relationship with your IT leader. Unlike your CEO, you don't have the option of replacing the person, so find some common ground.

- Don't wait for technologists to suggest new opportunities for technology use—do your own research and then leverage their knowledge. Technology is not just IT and product development's job—it's everyone's job.

- Find the "closet techie" in your own organization and encourage him to help educate you and your staff and to build relationships with IT. The latter can be a double-edged sword as IT organizations are sometimes defensive about someone invading their turf, so coach your team on how to make overtures without being obtrusive.

- Create an ongoing planning process that embeds technology staff into the formulation of plans and strategies.

Living Transformational Technology

Amazon is an exemplary user of technology for transformation. While originally pegged as an online retailer, Amazon moved into adjacent areas starting with providing infrastructure for other retailers, even competitors, to run online stores. It leveraged its expertise in running massive computing infrastructure to offer Amazon Web Services (AWS) and Elastic Compute Cloud (EC2) as product offerings.

Building on its book retailing experience and partnerships, it launched the Kindle, which in turn spawned a plethora of self-published books (including this one). In short, Amazon has a flexible and scalable platform of technology and business practices that allows it to continuously transform itself without having to "start over each time."

I'll leave you with some final thoughts about the role of technology strategy in energized enterprises. First, it isn't a department or function—it is everyone's job and should be part of the organization's

DNA. Second, technology is exciting and energizing—it opens up new horizons, new opportunities to learn, and new opportunities to serve customers in the ways that they desire. Finally, energized enterprises are continually searching for breakthrough technologies, but they do so with discipline and focus, heeding the quote at the beginning of this chapter.

In the next chapter, I'll provide some closing thoughts and a framework for creating your own energized enterprise.

Resources

- Denning, Steve. February 12, 2012. *Is Your IT Service Provider Delighting You?* Forbes.com.

- IBM Consulting Services. 2005. *Eliminating the Strategic Blind Spot.* IBM Corp.

- Roberts, Roger, and Johnson Sikes. 2011. *A Rising Role for IT.* McKinsey & Company.

- Simon, Phil. 2011. *The Age of the Platform.* Motion Publishing LLC.

- Vitalari, Nicholas, and Haydn Shaughnessy. 2012. *The Elastic Enterprise,* Telemachus Press.

CHAPTER 10

Now It's Your Turn: Start Your Engines

The year was 1969, and I was a youngster attending the Indy 500 auto race for the first time. Over the loudspeakers came the exhortation for racers to "start your engines." I'll never forget the sound of those powerful engines roaring to life. It was pure excitement, and truly inspiring for a fan like me.

Hopefully, the fact that you are reading this means that you are now inspired to start at least one of the eight engines discussed in this book—or, preferably, more than one. I've already provided advice about tackling each engine in their respective chapters, so here I'll summarize and highlight key takeaways for your journey to the energized enterprise.

A Framework for Change

Although I don't explicitly mention change much throughout the book, it is an implicit theme that is key to achieving an energized enterprise. The systems thinking discussion in Chapter 2 is germane to change, both in understanding its drivers and its unintended consequences.

I want to give you another framework that I've found useful in pursuing change management and organizational transformation initiatives, since creating an energized enterprise involves both. The framework in Figure 18 identifies primary factors that are involved in any significant organizational change, along with the needs of employees affected by the change.

Figure 18: Employee Needs in Energized Enterprise Achievement

Factor	Employee Needs
Relevance	Understand why they are being asked to change their behavior
Coherence	Understand the problem or opportunity and approach
Context	Understand why a change is being made
Support	Receive support and encouragement from management
Value	Receive appropriate value from changing behaviors
Reward	Receive reward for changing behaviors, preferably intrinsic

The framework provides a sequential model for identifying and addressing what employees need in order to embrace the changes described in the earlier chapters.

I've watched many organizational initiatives, even much-needed ones, fail because the implementers neglect to address one or more of the needs listed in Figure 18. If you are skeptical, try implementing a new computer application in your organization without explaining to users why they need to use it or how it will benefit them.

Now think about the adoption of that same application with some communication and support. For example:

"We're asking you to use this new system because it's crucial to the success of our business. Our production costs are not competitive in the global economy, and this system will help lower those costs so that we can be competitive. That's why we are asking you to learn this new system and some new ways of working.

"We recognize that learning this new system will take time and possibly even slow down your work in the short term, so we have put together a support team who will work with you until you are comfortable with the new processes. In talking with other users of this system, we found that it not only delivered cost efficiencies, but workers also preferred it because it eliminated process steps and workload. It also gives users more opportunities to contribute ideas for improving production processes, which we hope will make your jobs more satisfying."

The communication connects with all of the employeee needs or concerns and tackles them head on. Let's break it down:

1. Relevance: "We're asking you to use this new system because it's crucial to the success of our business."

2. Coherence: "Our production costs are not competitive in the global economy, and this system will help lower those costs so that we can be competitive."

3. Context: "That's why we are asking you to learn this new system and some new ways of working."

4. Support: "We recognize that learning this new system will take time and possibly even slow down your work in the short term, so we have put together a support team who will work with you until you are comfortable with the new processes."

5. Value: "In talking with other users of this system, we found that it not only delivered cost efficiencies, but workers also preferred it because it eliminated process steps and workload."

6. Reward: "It also gives users more opportunities to contribute ideas for improving production processes, which we hope will make your jobs more satisfying."

How to Start Your Energized Enterprise Journey

I sequenced the chapters of the book in the order that I would pursue creation of an energized enterprise. That's not to say that you need to follow the order religiously or even to implement all of the engines, but I do believe that the sequence is both logical and a positive reinforcing loop. As Figure 19 shows, the eight engines collectively form a virtuous circle or reinforcing loop.

Figure 19: The Virtuous Circle of Energizing Engines

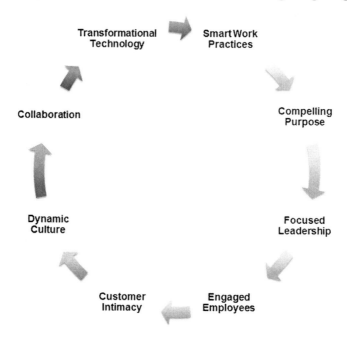

That means that progress made on each of the engines in turn drives progress in successive engines, and as an organization moves through the loop, energy levels rise until the organization becomes a 1+1=3 enterprise running on all cylinders.

My final to-do list consists of some thoughts about how to tackle energizing your enterprise:

Listen: It's said that a journey of a thousand miles begins with a single step, and for this journey, the first step is listening—really listening. Borrowing from *The X-Files*, "the truth is out there," and you only need to listen to find it. By listening, I don't mean relying on employee surveys or Q&A sessions. Get out among employees wherever you can and simply observe. (Take a cue from Marissa Mayer, who delighted

Yahoo employees by eating lunch in the cafeteria and attending Friday happy hours in the weeks after being named CEO.) Yes, it is OK to ask questions, but listen and observe first.

Chunk it Down: Tackling the journey as a whole is more than daunting. My best advice is to think globally and act locally. By that I mean that you should develop a big-picture view of what you plan to achieve, but then chunk it down into a series of projects or initiatives to actually make the journey. Unless you are a long-haul trucker, a cross-country trip involves a number of legs with rest stops in between. That's also true for the journey to an energized enterprise. The to-do lists in each chapter should provide a good starting point.

Get Systematic: The energizing journey has a lot of component parts and interactions. Adopting a systems thinking approach, as discussed in Chapter 2, will help manage the complexity of the journey and ensure that decisions aren't made in a vacuum. Your organization, regardless of size, is a complex system, and tinkering without understanding is like trying to defuse a bomb by randomly cutting wires. You might get lucky, but chances for that are slim. Invest the time and energy to get a solid baseline of where your organization stands. Each chapter in this book can help you assess your current state.

Call in Reinforcements: The reinforcing loop is a powerful construct and, used properly, will help propel your energizing journey. Energized enterprises are 1+1=3 organizations because each engine not only supplies its own energy but also feeds the other engines. Think about an organization with hard-working employees who are engaged in their tasks but lack understanding of the larger organization's purpose and how it serves its customers. Now take that same organization and add in a compelling purpose (Chapter 3) and customer intimacy (Chapter 6) and watch the sparks fly!

Get Agile: Creating an energized enterprise lends itself to an agile, iterative approach. Agile thinking helps build a continuous improvement culture that will, over time, lead to successful implementation of needed changes. Agile initiatives are self-reinforcing and self-correcting, so once you have agile DNA, it continues to spawn more agility—the classic reinforcing loop.

Lean Into Change: Several concepts drawn from lean thinking are germane to the energized enterprise journey, especially the notion of eliminating waste; i.e., anything that does not add value to a customer. Lean thinking can be a big help in deciding "how much is enough," whether used in process design, application development, or even marketing.

Don't Give Up: I've managed a lot of organizational change and I would say the most important ingredient for success is tenacity. If you ever watched films of Jack LaLanne pulling a bus with his teeth, you've seen what it can feel like to pull an organization through change. The good news is that your agile approach (you are using agile aren't you?) can mitigate the frustration by providing incremental evidence of progress and the energy to keep moving forward.

In closing, I sincerely hope that you find the personal energy and drive to create your own energized enterprise and that this book plays a role in inspiring and informing your journey. Life is short, and whatever your endeavors or those of your employees, they should take place in the favorable environment of an energized enterprise.

*   *   *

I'm interested in hearing about your experiences with following the advice in this book. Drop me a line at <u>mstrohlein@agilebusinesslogic.com</u> or follow me on Twitter: @mstrohlein.

ABOUT THE AUTHOR

Marc Strohlein is Principal at Agile Business Logic, a consultancy that helps small and medium-sized businesses, associations, and non-profits by optimizing their strategies, people, processes, and technologies *and* their interactions to create energized enterprises. He has over 30 years of experience as an executive, manager, and team leader in businesses ranging from startups to global corporations.

While often pegged as a "technology guy," Marc's real skill is in understanding the people side of technology—that nexus where the right blend and approach can create the magic of both enterprise systems that drive business performance and technology-driven products that yield profitable revenue streams. His passion and focus throughout his career have been in unlocking energy, focus, innovation, and growth in individuals, teams, and organizations.

Marc lives in the San Francisco Bay Area with his wife, Patricia.

He invites readers to e-mail him at mstrohlein@agilebusinesslogic.com, visit his website www.agilebusinesslogic.com, and follow him on Twitter: @mstrohlein.

CPSIA information can be obtained at www.ICGtesting.com
Printed in the USA
BVOW011143051212

307261BV00006B/249/P